C.99

THE SHAKESPEARE PARALLEL TEXT SERIES, THIRD EDITION

A Midsummer Night's Dream

by William Shakespeare

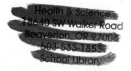

Perfection Learning© Corporation
Logan, Iowa 51546-0500

Editorial Director	Julie A. Schumacher
Senior Editor	Rebecca Christian
Series Editor	Rebecca Burke
Editorial Assistant	Kate Winzenburg
Writer, Modern Version	Janie B. Yates-Glandorf, Ph.D.
Design Director	Randy Messer
Design	Mark Hagenberg
Production	Word Designs
Art Research	Laura Wells
Cover Art	Brad Holland

PB ISBN-13: 978-0-7891-6085-4 ISBN-10: 0-7891-6085-0
RLB ISBN-13: 978-0-7569-1487-6 ISBN-10: 0-7569-1487-5
 7 8 9 10 11 PP 12 11 10 09

Table of Contents

A Midsummer Night's Dream . . 4

Timeline 10

Reading *A Midsummer*
    Night's Dream 11

Cast of Characters 15

Act 1

    Introduction 16

    Scene 1 20

    Scene 2 38

    Act I Review 48

Act 2

    Introduction 50

    Scene 1 54

    Scene 2 74

    Act II Review 86

Act 3

    Introduction 88

    Scene 1 92

    Scene 2 110

    Act III Review 148

Act 4

    Introduction 150

    Scene 1 154

    Scene 2 172

    Act IV Review 176

Act 5

    Introduction 178

    Scene 1 182

    Act V Review 216

The Play in Review 218

Shakespeare's Life 222

Shakespeare's Theater 226

The Globe Theatre 230

A *Midsummer Night's Dream*

Magic, song and dance, fairies, lovers, and surprisingly serious insights into our secret emotional lives. What's not to love about the fast-paced gaiety that is *A Midsummer Night's Dream*? Not much, according to audiences, who have long made it the most popular of Shakespeare's comedies.

Shakespeare conjured up this tale of summer love gone wrong and then righted again as one of a glorious string of comedies in about 1595. Scholars think he probably wrote it soon after his early tragedy, *Romeo and Juliet*, the plot of which echoes throughout this frisky comedy. As in *Romeo and Juliet*, the play features a young couple in love, their disapproving elders, secret meetings, and a flight from authority. But where *Romeo and Juliet* is heartbreaking, *A Midsummer Night's Dream* is lighthearted, even burlesque. It includes Shakespeare's most famous scenes of low comedy, complete with cross-dressing and a regal Fairy Queen falling madly in love with a bumbling actor wearing a donkey's head. When she comes to her senses, the Queen speaks one of the most famous lines in the history of comedy, "Methought I was enamour'd of an ass."

Shakespeare's Sources

Setting his comedy in ancient Athens and the woods nearby, Shakespeare energetically wove the story together from literary odds and ends. He borrowed the characters Theseus and Hippolyta from Greek mythology; their story is chronicled in both Chaucer's *Knight's Tale* and Plutarch's *Lives*. In myth, the hero Theseus conquers the Amazonians and wins their queen, Hippolyta. *A Midsummer Night's Dream* begins in Athens with the two about to be married when Egeus, an Athenian, comes to complain to Theseus about his daughter, Hermia, whom he has promised in marriage to a young man named Demetrius. Unfortunately, Hermia loves another, Lysander. When Theseus demands that Hermia either obey her father or face severe punishment or death, she and Lysander flee to the woods near Athens. They are followed by Demetrius, in turn pursued by another young woman, Helena, who loves him although he loves her not.

A high school production of *A Midsummer Night's Dream*

In the woods, members of the fairy kingdom have gathered to celebrate the royal wedding. As the fairies distribute spells, merry complications among the lovers ensue, leading to one of the most well-known quotes from the play, "The course of true love never did run smooth." Shakespeare blended medieval English folklore with that of his own time to create the whimsical leader of the fairies, Puck. Until Shakespeare transformed him, Puck had been depicted as an evil spirit. Shakespeare took Puck out of the dark and menacing forest and brought him into the sunlight by linking him with Robin Goodfellow. Robin was a gentle spirit thought by some to haunt the dappled Forest of Arden near Shakespeare's home. Whatever his mood, troublemaking or helpful, Puck is a reminder that the fairy world is not a place where predictable, natural laws prevail.

Puck, a painting by Sir Joshua Reynolds, 18th century

Satirizing Styles

It was once thought that Shakespeare wrote the comedy to celebrate an aristocratic wedding. Most scholars today discount this idea, but they do compare it to a form of entertainment popular in Shakespearean times—the masque. A masque was a court drama with stylized music and dances, elaborate speeches, and supernatural characters.

In his comedy, Shakespeare satirized the way Elizabethan tragedy was so often presented, with long-winded speeches and expressions of sorrow. To create a comic play within his play, he mined Ovid's serious work *Metamorphoses*. The result is the rollicking "tragical comedy" of Pyramus and Thisbe, which turns Ovid's account of star-crossed lovers on its head. Shakespeare's cartoonish version is entitled "The most lamentable comedy, and most cruel death of Pyramus and Thisbe."

In it, the "hero" Pyramus drags out his death scene as he staggers around the stage hollering "Thus die I, thus, thus, thus. / Now I am dead; / Now I am fled . . . Now die, die, die, die, die." Just as Hamlet's "to be or not to be" scene is coveted by Shakespearean actors specializing in tragedy, Pyramus's dying scene in this play has been fought over by centuries of hams. It is interesting to note that the play within the play parallels both the larger comedy in which it is imbedded and *Romeo and Juliet*. Like Romeo, Pyramus kills himself because he mistakenly thinks his lover is dead; like Juliet, Thisbe does likewise when she learns how her lover has come to grief.

Magic, Mood, and Metaphor

A Midsummer Night's Dream has been described as a fairy tale for adults. It has poetic images ("I must go seek some dewdrops here, / And hang a pearl in every cowslip's ear."). It has a happy ending ("Here come the lovers, full of joy and mirth."). Magic is used as a metaphor for romantic love, which is portrayed as temporary madness heightened by the imagination and buoyed by the summer breeze. Theseus says that the lunatic, the poet, and the lover are all driven by imagination—the madman sees devils; the lover sees beauty where it does not exist; and

William Hurt as Oberon (center, top) and the rest of the cast in 1982 production at the New York Shakespeare Festival, produced by Joseph Papp, directed by Joseph Lapine

the poet's pen gives form to "airy nothing." He adds that even in the best play, the characters are merely shadows, hinting that the same could be said of all humans and perhaps of life itself. It is not an accident that Shakespeare had his intertwined love stories take place on Midsummer Day, a festival associated with love, fertility—and a free pass from the mundane responsibilities of daily life.

Contrasts abound in *A Midsummer Night's Dream*, contrasts between night and day, the formality of the city and the sensuality of the woods, reality and appearance, royalty and the rough working class. Some scholars believe the fairies represent natural forces, even insisting that the Fairy Queen's affair with Bottom, who wears an ass's head, represents bestiality. It is interesting to note that many directors double cast Theseus and Hippolyta as Oberon and Titania. Of course, there are practical reasons for this, but the directors may also be acknowledging that most humans have in their make-up elements of both the practical and fanciful. Ultimately the humans represent law and reason—after their spree in the woods, the lovers return to the city to be safely married.

From title to text, dreams both waking and sleeping play an important role in this thoughtful comedy. They underline the notion that humankind's deepest truths are buried in the subconscious. Only on rare occasions do dreams offer a glimpse into the psyche's moon-drenched depths. The play ends with Puck saying that if "we shadows"—the characters—have given offense, the audience members should imagine that they have been sleeping and consider the play only a dream.

Timeline

1564	Shakespeare is baptized.
1568	Elizabeth I becomes Queen of England.
1572	Shakespeare begins grammar school.
1576	Opening of The Theatre, the first permanent playhouse in England.
1580	Drake sails around the world.
1582	Shakespeare marries Anne Hathaway.
1583	Shakespeare's daughter Susanna is baptized.
1585	Shakespeare's twins are baptized.
1588	Spanish Armada is defeated.
1592-94	Plague closes all of London's theaters.
1594	*Titus Andronicus* becomes first printed Shakespeare play.
1594	Shakespeare joins the Lord Chamberlain's Men.
1599	Lord Chamberlain's Men build the Globe Theatre; Shakespeare is part-owner of the building.
1609	Shakespeare's *Sonnets* published for the first time.
1610	Shakespeare retires to Stratford.
1613	Globe Theatre burns to the ground.
1616	William Shakespeare dies at the age of 52.
1623	Shakespeare's wife dies.
	First Folio published.

Reading *A Midsummer Night's Dream*

Using This Parallel Text

This edition of *A Midsummer Night's Dream* is especially designed for readers who aren't familiar with Shakespeare. If you're fairly comfortable with his language, simply read the original text on the left-hand page. When you come to a confusing word or passage, refer to the modern English version on the right or the footnotes at the bottom.

If you think Elizabethan English doesn't even sound like English, read a passage of the modern version silently. Then read the same passage of the original. You'll find that Shakespeare's language begins to come alive for you. You may choose to work your way through the entire play this way.

As you read more, you'll probably find yourself using the modern version less and less. Remember, the parallel version is meant to be an aid, not a substitute for the original. If you read only the modern version, you'll cheat yourself out of Shakespeare's language—his quick-witted puns, sharp-tongued insults, and evocative images.

Keep in mind that language is a living thing, constantly growing and changing. New words are invented and new definitions for old words are added. Since Shakespeare wrote over four hundred years ago, it is not surprising that his work seems challenging to today's readers.

Here are some other reading strategies that can increase your enjoyment of the play.

Background

Knowing some historical background makes it easier to understand what's going on. You will find more about Shakespeare's life and Elizabethan theater at the back of the book. Reading the summaries that precede each act will also help you to follow the action of the play.

Getting the Beat

Like most dramatists of his time, Shakespeare frequently used **blank verse** in his plays. In blank verse, the text is written in measured lines that do not rhyme. Look at the following example from *A Midsummer Night's Dream*.

> Tomorrow night when Phoebe doth behold
> Her silver visage in the wat'ry glass,
> Decking with liquid pearl the bladed grass
> A time that lovers' flights doth still conceal . . .

You can see that the four lines above are approximately equal in length, but they do not cover the whole width of the page as the lines in a story or essay might. They are, in fact, unrhymed verse with each line containing ten or eleven syllables. Furthermore, the ten syllables can be divided into five sections, called **iambs,** or feet. Each iamb contains one unstressed (**U**) and one stressed (**/**) syllable. Try reading the lines below, giving emphasis to the capitalized syllable in each iamb.

U /	U /	U /	U /	U /
ToMOR	row NIGHT	when PHOE	be DOTH	beHOLD

U /	U /	U /	U /	U /
Her SIL	ver VIS	age IN	the WAT	'ry GLASS, . . .

The length of a line of verse is measured by counting the stresses. This length is known as the **meter,** and when there are five stresses and the rhythm follows an unstressed/stressed pattern, it is known as **iambic pentameter.** Much of Shakespeare's work is written in iambic pentameter.

Of course, Shakespeare was not rigid about this format. He sometimes varied the lines by putting accents in unusual places, by having lines with more or fewer than ten syllables, and by varying where pauses occur. An actor's interpretation can also add variety. (Only a terrible actor would deliver lines in a way that makes the rhythm sound singsong!)

Prose

In addition to verse, Shakespeare wrote speeches in **prose**, or language without rhythmic structure. Look at the comical tradesmen's speech in Act III, Scene i. If you try beating out an iambic rhythm to these lines, you'll discover that it doesn't work because they're in prose. But once Titania, Queen of the Fairies, awakes and starts speaking, you'll be able to find the rhythm of iambic pentameter again. Shakespeare often uses prose for comic speeches, to show madness, and for characters of lower social rank such as servants. His upper-class characters generally do not speak in prose. But these weren't hard and fast rules as far as Shakespeare was concerned. Whether characters speak in verse or prose is often a function of the situation and whom they're addressing, as well as their social status.

Contractions

As you know, contractions are words that have been combined by substituting an apostrophe for a letter or letters that have been removed. Contractions were as common in Shakespeare's time as they are today. For example, we use *it's* as a contraction for the words *it is*. In Shakespeare's writing you will discover that *'tis* means the same thing. Shakespeare often used the apostrophe to shorten words so that they would fit into the rhythmic pattern of a line. This is especially true of verbs ending in *-ed*. Note that in Shakespeare's plays, the *-ed* at the end of a verb is usually pronounced as a separate syllable. Therefore, *walked* would be pronounced as two syllables, *walk*ed*, while *walk'd* would be only one.

Speak and Listen

Remember that plays are written to be acted, not read silently. Reading out loud—whether in a group or alone—helps you to "hear" the meaning. Listening to another reader will also help. You might also enjoy listening to a recording of the play by professional actors.

Clues and Cues

Shakespeare was sparing in his use of stage directions. In fact, many of those in modern editions were added by later editors. Added stage directions are usually indicated by brackets. For example, [aside] tells the actor to give the audience information that the other characters can't hear.

The Play's the Thing

Finally, if you can't figure out every word in the play, don't get discouraged. The people in Shakespeare's audience couldn't either. At that time, language was changing rapidly and standardized spelling, punctuation, grammar, and even dictionaries did not exist. Besides, Shakespeare loved to play with words. He made up new combinations, like *fat-guts* and *mumble-news*. To make matters worse, the actors probably spoke very rapidly. But the audience didn't strain to catch every word. They went to a Shakespeare play for the same reasons we go to a movie—to get caught up in the story and the acting, to have a great laugh or a good cry.

Cast of Characters

HERMIA
LYSANDER
HELENA
DEMETRIUS
} four lovers

THESEUS Duke of Athens
HIPPOLYTA Queen of the Amazons
EGEUS father to Hermia
PHILOSTRATE master of the revels to Theseus

NICK BOTTOM weaver
PETER QUINCE carpenter
FRANCIS FLUTE bellows-mender
TOM SNOUT tinker
SNUG joiner
ROBIN STARVELING tailor

OBERON King of the Fairies
TITANIA Queen of the Fairies
ROBIN GOODFELLOW a "puck," or hobgoblin, in Oberon's service
A FAIRY in the service of Titania
PEASEBLOSSOM
COBWEB
MOTH
MUSTARDSEED
} fairies attending upon Titania

LORDS and **ATTENDANTS** on Theseus and Hippolyta
OTHER FAIRIES in the trains of Titania and Oberon

A Midsummer Night's Dream

ACT I

Egeus and the lovers before Theseus and Hippolyta, 1932 film directed by William Dieterle and Max Reinhardt

*"The course of true love
never did run smooth."*

Before You Read

1. The action of the play you are about to read takes place in four days. Consider some books and movies where the story unfolds quickly. What elements do you think might be necessary for such a compressed tale to succeed?

2. This comedy takes place in midsummer. What three words would you use to describe the middle of the summer?

3. What does the use of the word "dream" in the title lead you to expect from the play?

4. *A Midsummer Night's Dream* is sometimes described as a fairy tale for adults. What are some of the characteristics of a fairy tale?

Literary Elements

1. A **soliloquy** is a long speech that reveals the innermost thoughts and feelings of the character who speaks it. In Helena's soliloquy at the end of Scene i, she tells of her love for Demetrius and outlines a plan to win him.

2. Shakespeare often uses **repetition** to stress a character's emotions or traits or lend urgency to a theme or idea. In Act I, Scene i, Lysander would like to remove Demetrius, a rival suitor, from competition for his Hermia's hand. He claims that a different woman, Helena, loves Demetrius and exaggerates her love for him by repeating the word "dotes": "and she, sweet lady, dotes, / Devoutly dotes, dotes in idolatry."

3. An **oxymoron** is a combination of contradictory words. In this play, Nick Bottom promises to "roar gently" when he plays the part of a lion.

4. **Titles** are an important element of plays. The title *A Midsummer Night's Dream* conveys a tone and gives information about when this play takes place and what it's about.

Words to Know

The following vocabulary words appear in Act I in the original text of Shakespeare's play. However, they are words that are still used today. Read the definitions here and pay attention to the words as you read the play (they will be in boldfaced type).

abjure	give up; surrender
austerity	harshness; severity
cloister	convent; sheltered place
discretion	good sense; taste
edict	order; decree
enthralled [enthrall'd]	thrilled; taken in by
extenuate	lessen; make less serious
idolatry	worship; extreme devotion
nuptial	related to a wedding
revelling	celebrating
solemnities	ceremonies; serious occasions
transpose	change; switch
vexation	trouble; irritation
wanes	fades; becomes weaker

Act Summary

Theseus, Duke of Athens, plans to marry Hippolyta, the Queen of the Amazons, whom he has defeated in battle. Their wedding is four days away. As Theseus eagerly prepares for his wedding, Egeus, a nobleman, comes to visit. Egeus is troubled because he has promised his daughter Hermia in marriage to a young man named Demetrius, but Hermia loves another young man, Lysander.

Theseus permits Egeus to invoke an ancient law that says a man's daughter must marry the person her father chooses. If she refuses, she must either become a nun or be put to death.

After Theseus outlines these unhappy choices to Hermia, her lover, Lysander, persuades her to steal away into the forest near Athens with him the next day and marry him. Lysander departs, and Hermia's girlhood friend Helena comes to visit her. Helena is miserable because

The workmen/actors, Royal Shakespeare Company, 1989 production, Stratford-upon-Avon

she is in love with Hermia's unwanted suitor, Demetrius, who once loved her. Hermia consoles her friend by telling her that she isn't going to marry Demetrius and instead secretly plans to marry Lysander. Helena betrays Hermia by tipping Demetrius off to the lovers' plan. She hopes that when Demetrius follows them into the forest, the sight of Hermia in Lysander's arms will make him return to her.

Meanwhile, a troupe of amateur actors—rough and uneducated workmen, known as the mechanicals—are rehearsing a badly written play. They hope to perform it as part of the Duke's wedding festivities.

ACT I, SCENE I

[*Athens. the Palace of Theseus.*] *Enter* THESEUS, HIPPOLYTA, *and* PHILOSTRATE, *with others.*

THESEUS

Now, fair Hippolyta, our **nuptial** hour
Draws on apace. Four happy days bring in
Another moon; but, O, methinks, how slow
This old moon **wanes**! She lingers my desires,
5   Like to a stepdame or a dowager
Long withering out a young man's revenue.

HIPPOLYTA

Four days will quickly steep themselves in night;
Four nights will quickly dream away the time;
And then the moon, like to a silver bow
10   New-bent in heaven, shall behold the night
Of our **solemnities**.

THESEUS

              Go, Philostrate,
Stir up the Athenian youth to merriments;
Awake the pert and nimble spirit of mirth;
15   Turn melancholy forth to funerals.
The pale companion is not for our pomp.

[*Exit* PHILOSTRATE.]

Hippolyta, I woo'd thee with my sword,*
And won thy love doing thee injuries;
But I will wed thee in another key,
20   With pomp, with triumph, and with **revelling**.

Enter EGEUS, HERMIA, LYSANDER, *and* DEMETRIUS.

EGEUS

Happy be Theseus, our renowned Duke!

---

17   *woo'd thee with my sword* Theseus captured Hippolyta, the Amazon queen, when he conquered the Amazons.

ACT 1, SCENE 1

The palace of Theseus. THESEUS, HIPPOLYTA, PHILOSTRATE, *and* OTHERS *enter.*

THESEUS
Now, beautiful Hippolyta, our wedding hour
quickly approaches. In four happy days we'll see
another moon, but, oh, how slowly
the old moon fades. She prolongs my desires
like a stepmother or a widow   5
who drains away a young man's income.

HIPPOLYTA
Four days will quickly become immersed in night.
Four nights will quickly dream away the time,
and then the moon, like a silver bow
newly bent in heaven, will witness the night   10
of our wedding ceremony.

THESEUS
Go, Philostrate,
stir up the young people of Athens to festivities.
Wake up the lively and nimble spirit of fun.
Show melancholy the way to the funerals.   15
That sad fellow is not welcome at our happy festival.

> PHILOSTRATE *exits.*

Hippolyta, I pursued you with my sword,
and I won your love as I was giving you injury.
But I will marry you in a different tone,
with ceremony, pageantry, and celebration.   20

> EGEUS *enters with his daughter* HERMIA, LYSANDER, *and*
> DEMETRIUS.

EGEUS
I wish you happiness, Theseus, our famous Duke.

THESEUS

Thanks, good Egeus. What's the news with thee?

EGEUS

Full of **vexation** come I, with complaint
Against my child, my daughter Hermia.—
25   Stand forth, Demetrius.—My noble lord,
This man hath my consent to marry her.—
Stand forth, Lysander.—And, my gracious duke,
This man hath bewitch'd the bosom of my child.—
Thou, thou, Lysander, thou hast given her rhymes
30   And interchang'd love-tokens with my child.
Thou hast by moonlight at her window sung
With feigning voice verses of feigning love,
And stol'n the impression of her fantasy
With bracelets of thy hair, rings, gawds, conceits,
35   Knacks, trifles, nosegays, sweetmeats—messengers
Of strong prevailment in unharden'd youth.
With cunning hast thou filch'd my daughter's heart,
Turn'd her obedience, which is due to me,
To stubborn harshness;—and, my gracious Duke,
40   Be it so she will not here before your Grace
Consent to marry with Demetrius,
I beg the ancient privilege of Athens:
As she is mine, I may dispose of her;
Which shall be either to this gentleman
45   Or to her death, according to our law
Immediately provided in that case.

THESEUS

What say you, Hermia? Be advis'd, fair maid.
To you your father should be as a god,
One that compos'd your beauties, yea, and one
50   To whom you are but as a form in wax
By him imprinted, and within his power
To leave the figure or disfigure it.
Demetrius is a worthy gentleman.

HERMIA

So is Lysander.

THESEUS

Thank you, good Egeus. What's your news?

EGEUS

I come to you full of troubles. I have a complaint
against my child, my daughter Hermia.—
Come here, Demetrius.—My noble lord,   25
this man has my consent to marry her.—
Come here, Lysander.—And my gracious lord,
this man has ensnared the heart of my child.—
You, you, Lysander, you have given her poems
and you have exchanged tokens of love with my child.   30
At moonlight by her window, you've sung
seductive long poems in a seductive voice.
You have deviously captured her imagination
with bracelets of your hair, rings, trinkets, clever baubles,
knickknacks, trifles, flowers, candy—all messengers   35
of strong persuasion for an innocent young woman.
With cunning you have stolen my daughter's heart
and turned the obedience due to me
to stubborn harshness.—So, my gracious Duke,
if she will not consent, here before you, your Grace,   40
to agree to marry Demetrius,
I beg to be granted the ancient privilege of Athens.
That states that since she is mine, I can deliver her
either to this gentleman (*Demetrius*)
or to her death, according to the law   45
which is expressly granted in this case.

THESEUS

What do you say, Hermia? Listen to me, lovely maiden:
To you, your father should be like a god,
one who created your beauty. Yes, and one
to whom you are just a wax form   50
which he shaped and which he can
leave untouched or destroy.
Demetrius is a worthy gentleman.

HERMIA

So is Lysander.

THESEUS

₅₅　　　　　　　　　In himself he is;
But in this kind, wanting your father's voice,
The other must be held the worthier.

HERMIA

I would my father look'd but with my eyes.

THESEUS

Rather your eyes must with his judgment look.

HERMIA

₆₀　I do entreat your Grace to pardon me.
I know not by what power I am made bold,
Nor how it may concern my modesty
In such a presence here to plead my thoughts;
But I beseech your Grace that I may know
₆₅　The worst that may befall me in this case
If I refuse to wed Demetrius.

THESEUS

Either to die the death or to **abjure**
For ever the society of men.
Therefore, fair Hermia, question your desires,
₇₀　Know of your youth, examine well your blood,
Whether, if you yield not to your father's choice,
You can endure the livery of a nun,
For aye to be in shady **cloister** mew'd,
To live a barren sister all your life,
₇₅　Chanting faint hymns to the cold fruitless moon.
Thrice-blessed they that master so their blood
To undergo such maiden pilgrimage;
But earthlier happy is the rose distill'd
Than that which withering on the virgin thorn,
₈₀　Grows, lives, and dies in single blessedness.

HERMIA

So will I grow, so live, so die, my lord,
Ere I will yield my virgin patent up
Unto his lordship, whose unwished yoke
My soul consents not to give sovereignty.

THESEUS

Yes, in himself he his.   55
But in this case, since your father does not approve of him,
the other man must be considered worthier.

HERMIA

I only wish my father could see with my eyes.

THESEUS

To the contrary, you must judge things from his viewpoint.

HERMIA

I beg your Grace to pardon me.   60
I don't know what influence makes me so bold,
or how it will compromise my reputation for modesty
to plead for my thoughts in such company.
But, I beg you, your Grace, that I may know
the worst that can happen to me in this situation   65
if I refuse to marry Demetrius.

THESEUS

You must either die or give up
forever the society of men.
Therefore, beautiful Hermia, closely examine your desires,
think about your youth, examine your passions.   70
Decide whether or not, if you don't choose the man your father
     favors,
you can stand to wear the clothing of a nun.
You will be shut up in a dark convent forever
to live as a childless sister all your life,
chanting weak hymns to the cold, childless moon.   75
Three-times blessed are those who can control their passions to
     such a degree
and choose such a virginal route.
But the rose that is picked for perfume is happier in earthly terms
than the rose that withers on the untouched vine—
which grows, lives, and dies in lonely purity.   80

HERMIA

Then that is the way I will grow, live, and die, my lord,
before I will give up my right to virginity
and put it in the hands of that lord to whose unwelcome proposal
my soul will not consent to acknowledge as my master.

THESEUS

85 Take time to pause; and, by the next new moon—
The sealing-day betwixt my love and me
For everlasting bond of fellowship—
Upon that day either prepare to die
For disobedience to your father's will,

90 Or else to wed Demetrius, as he would,
Or on Diana's altar to protest
For aye **austerity** and single life.

DEMETRIUS

Relent, sweet Hermia; and, Lysander, yield
Thy crazed title to my certain right.

LYSANDER

95 You have her father's love, Demetrius,
Let me have Hermia's; do you marry him.

EGEUS

Scornful Lysander, true, he hath my love;
And what is mine my love shall render him.
And she is mine, and all my right of her

100 I do estate unto Demetrius.

LYSANDER [*to* THESEUS]

I am, my lord, as well deriv'd as he,
As well possess'd. My love is more than his;
My fortunes every way as fairly rank'd,
If not with vantage, as Demetrius's;

105 And, which is more than all these boasts can be,
I am belov'd of beauteous Hermia.
Why should not I then prosecute my right?
Demetrius, I'll avouch it to his head,
Made love to Nedar's daughter, Helena,

110 And won her soul; and she, sweet lady, dotes,
Devoutly dotes, dotes in **idolatry**,
Upon this spotted and inconstant man.

THESEUS

I must confess that I have heard so much,
And with Demetrius thought to have spoke thereof;

115 But, being overfull of self-affairs,
My mind did lose it.—But, Demetrius, come,

THESEUS

Take time to think it over, and by the next new moon—   85
the day my love and I will seal our love
in the everlasting bond of marriage—
upon that day, either prepare to die
for disobeying your father's orders,
or else marry Demetrius as your father wishes.   90
If not, you must vow on Diana's altar
to live forever an austere and unmarried life.

DEMETRIUS

Give in, sweet Hermia. Lysander, give up
your weak claim to my undeniable right.

LYSANDER

You have her father's love, Demetrius.   95
Let me have Hermia's. You can marry him.

EGEUS

Scornful Lysander! You're right, I do love him;
and my love shall give him what is mine.
And Hermia is mine, and all my rights to her,
I give to Demetrius.   100

LYSANDER (*to* THESEUS)

My lord, my family is as noble as his,
and just as rich; my love is greater than his.
My fortunes are in every way equal,
if not better, than Demetrius's.
And what is more important than all of these boasts is that   105
I am loved by the beautiful Hermia.
Why shouldn't I claim my rights then?
I will swear it to his face that Demetrius
made love to Nedar's daughter, Helena,
and won her heart. And she, sweet lady, adores him—   110
devoutly adores him, adores him to the point of idolizing him—
this immortal and unfaithful man.

THESEUS

I must confess that I have heard that,
and I had meant to speak with Demetrius about it.
But, being overly concerned with my own affairs,   115
I forgot. But come, Demetrius,

And come, Egeus; you shall go with me.
I have some private schooling for you both.—
For you, fair Hermia, look you arm yourself
120 To fit your fancies to your father's will,
Or else the law of Athens yields you up—
Which by no means we may **extenuate**—
To death or to a vow of single life.—
Come, my Hippolyta; what cheer, my love?—
125 Demetrius and Egeus, go along.
I must employ you in some business
Against our nuptial, and confer with you
Of something nearly that concerns yourselves.

EGEUS

With duty and desire we follow you.

[*Exeunt all but* LYSANDER *and* HERMIA.]

LYSANDER

130 How now, my love! Why is your cheek so pale?
How chance the roses there do fade so fast?

HERMIA

Belike for want of rain, which I could well
Beteem them from the tempest of my eyes.

LYSANDER

Ay me! For aught that I could ever read,
135 Could ever hear by tale or history,
The course of true love never did run smooth.
But either it was different in blood—

HERMIA

O cross! Too high to be **enthrall'd** to low.

LYSANDER

Or else misgraffed in respect of years—

HERMIA

140 O spite! Too old to be engag'd to young.

LYSANDER

Or else it stood upon the choice of friends—

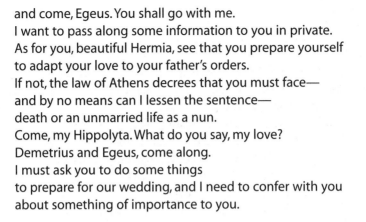

and come, Egeus. You shall go with me.
I want to pass along some information to you in private.
As for you, beautiful Hermia, see that you prepare yourself
to adapt your love to your father's orders.   120
If not, the law of Athens decrees that you must face—
and by no means can I lessen the sentence—
death or an unmarried life as a nun.
Come, my Hippolyta. What do you say, my love?
Demetrius and Egeus, come along.   125
I must ask you to do some things
to prepare for our wedding, and I need to confer with you
about something of importance to you.

EGEUS

We follow you with eager obedience.

All exit, except LYSANDER *and* HERMIA.

LYSANDER

What's wrong, my love? Why are you so pale?   130
Why do the roses fade so fast from your cheeks?

HERMIA

Perhaps it is for lack of rain, which I could easily
give them with a storm from my eyes.

LYSANDER

Alas! Nothing that i have ever read
or have ever heard from stories and from history   135
said that the course of true love runs smoothly.
But either because of a difference in rank—

HERMIA

Oh, what a misfortune! Too noble to be enslaved by such a
humble lover!

LYSANDER

Or else to be mismatched in terms of age—

HERMIA

Oh spite! Too old to be engaged to one so young!   140

LYSANDER

Or else because of the opinion of friends—

HERMIA

O hell! To choose love by another's eyes.

LYSANDER

Or, if there were a sympathy in choice,
War, death, or sickness did lay siege to it,
145 Making it momentany as a sound,
Swift as a shadow, short as any dream,
Brief as the lightning in the collied night,
That, in a spleen, unfolds both heaven and earth,
And ere a man hath power to say "Behold!"
150 The jaws of darkness do devour it up.
So quick bright things come to confusion.

HERMIA

If then true lovers have been ever cross'd,
It stands as an **edict** in destiny.
Then let us teach our trial patience,
155 Because it is a customary cross,
As due to love as thoughts and dreams and sighs,
Wishes and tears, poor fancy's followers.

LYSANDER

A good persuasion; therefore, hear me, Hermia.
I have a widow aunt, a dowager
160 Of great revenue, and she hath no child.
From Athens is her house remote seven leagues;
And she respects me as her only son.
There, gentle Hermia, may I marry thee;
And to that place the sharp Athenian law
165 Cannot pursue us. If thou lov'st me then,
Steal forth thy father's house tomorrow night;
And in the wood, a league without the town,
Where I did meet thee once with Helena
To do observance to a morn of May,
170 There will I stay for thee.

HERMIA

My good Lysander!

HERMIA

Oh hell! To choose a lover by someone else's standards!

LYSANDER

Or else if they are well-matched,
war, death, or sickness would seize it
and make it as momentary as a sound,   145
as swift as a shadow, as short as any dream,
or as brief as lightning on a dark night
that in a flash, reveals both heaven and earth.
And before a man has the power to say "Behold,"
the jaws of darkness have swallowed it.   150
Just in that manner do all quick, bright things come to a dark end.

HERMIA

If true lovers have always been afflicted,
it is because fate orders it.
So let us learn to be patient in our suffering
because suffering is a normal cross to bear.   155
It is as much a part of love as thoughts and dreams and sighs,
and wishes and tears—poor love's followers.

LYSANDER

That's a wise point of view. So listen, Hermia.
I have a widowed aunt, an heiress
with a large income and no children.   160
Her house is about twenty-one miles from Athens,
and she thinks of me as her only son.
There, gentle Hermia, I can marry you.
There the strict Athenian law
cannot follow us. If you love me, then,   165
sneak out of your father's house tomorrow night.
In the woods, about three miles outside of town,
where I once met you with Helena
to take part in the May Day celebration,
I will wait for you.   170

HERMIA

My good Lysander!

I swear to thee, by Cupid's* strongest bow,
By his best arrow with the golden head,
By the simplicity of Venus's doves,
175 By that which knitteth souls and prospers loves,
And by that fire which burn'd the Carthage queen*
When the false Troyan under sail was seen,
By all the vows that ever men have broke,
In number more than ever women spoke,
180 In that same place thou hast appointed me
Tomorrow truly will I meet with thee.

LYSANDER
Keep promise, love. Look, here comes Helena.

Enter HELENA.

HERMIA
God speed fair Helena! Whither away?

HELENA
Call you me "fair"? That "fair" again unsay.
185 Demetrius loves your fair. O happy fair!
Your eyes are lodestars, and your tongue's sweet air
More tuneable than lark to shepherd's ear
When wheat is green, when hawthorn buds appear.
Sickness is catching; O, were favour so,
190 Yours would I catch, fair Hermia, ere I go.
My ear should catch your voice, my eye your eye;
My tongue should catch your tongue's sweet melody.
Were the world mine, Demetrius being bated,
The rest I'll give to be to you translated.
195 O, teach me how you look, and with what art
You sway the motion of Demetrius's heart.

HERMIA
I frown upon him, yet he loves me still.

HELENA
O that your frowns would teach my smiles such skill!

---

172 *Cupid* Roman god of love. Struck by one of Cupid's gold-tipped arrows, a man or woman immediately fell in love. A lead-tipped arrow caused hate.

176 *Carthage queen* Dido, who committed suicide when she saw that Aeneas, her lover, had left her

I swear to you, by Cupid's strongest bow,
by his best arrow with the golden head,
by the innocence of Venus' doves,
by that which binds up souls and furthers love,   175
and by the fire which burned the Carthage queen
when that fickle Trojan Aeneas set sail—
by all the vows that men have ever broken,
which are more numerous than women have ever spoken,
in that place that you have set for meeting me,   180
I swear I'll meet you tomorrow.

LYSANDER

Keep your promise, love. Look, here comes Helena.

      HELENA *enters.*

HERMIA

God bless you, lovely Helena. Where are you going?

HELENA

Do you call me beautiful? Take back that "beautiful."
Demetrius loves your beauty. Oh happy beautiful one!   185
Your eyes are guiding stars, and your voice is sweet music,
more tuneful than a lark to a shepherd's ear
when wheat is green and hawthorn buds appear.
Sickness is catching. Oh, if only looks were catching,
I would catch yours, Hermia, before I left!   190
My ear would catch your voice, my eye would catch your eye,
my tongue would catch your voice's sweet melody.
If all the world were mine, except for Demetrius,
I'd give it all to be changed into you.
Oh, teach me to look like you and the tricks   195
with which you captured Demetrius's heart!

HERMIA

I frown at him, yet he still loves me.

HELENA

I wish your frowns could teach my smiles such skill!

HERMIA

I give him curses, yet he gives me love.

HELENA

200   O that my prayers could such affection move!

HERMIA

The more I hate, the more he follows me.

HELENA

The more I love, the more he hateth me.

HERMIA

His folly, Helena, is no fault of mine.

HELENA

None, but your beauty. Would that fault were mine!

HERMIA

205   Take comfort: he no more shall see my face;
Lysander and myself will fly this place.
Before the time I did Lysander see,
Seem'd Athens as a paradise to me.
O, then, what graces in my love do dwell,
210   That he hath turn'd a heaven unto a hell!

LYSANDER

Helen, to you our minds we will unfold.
Tomorrow night when Phoebe* doth behold
Her silver visage in the wat'ry glass,
Decking with liquid pearl the bladed grass,
215   A time that lovers' flights doth still conceal,
Through Athens' gates have we devis'd to steal.

HERMIA

And in the wood, where often you and I
Upon faith primrose beds were wont to lie,
Emptying our bosoms of their counsel sweet.
220   There my Lysander and myself shall meet;
And thence from Athens turn away our eyes,
To seek new friends and stranger companies.
Farewell, sweet playfellow! Pray thou for us,
And good luck grant thee thy Demetrius!—

---

212   *Phoebe* the goddess of the moon

HERMIA

I give him curses, yet he gives me love.

HELENA

I wish my prayers could win me such affection! 200

HERMIA

The more I hate him, the more he follows me.

HELENA

The more I love him, the more he hates me.

HERMIA

Helena, his foolishness is not my fault.

HELENA

No—except for your beauty. I wish I had that fault!

HERMIA

Take comfort. He shall not see my face again. 205
Lysander and I are going to flee from this place.
Before I met Lysander,
Athens seemed like a paradise to me.
But my lover is filled with such graces
that he has turned a heaven into a hell. 210

LYSANDER

Helen, we will tell you our secret plans.
Tomorrow night, when Phoebe can see
her silvery face in the water's mirror
and she dresses the blades of grass in liquid pearls,
—a time when lovers' flights are always hidden— 215
we are going to sneak out of Athens' gates.

HERMIA

And in the woods, where often you and I
used to lie upon pale primrose beds
telling each other everything in our secret hearts,
Lysander and I will meet. 220
We shall turn our eyes away from Athens
and find new friends among strangers.
Good-bye, sweet playmate. Pray for us.
And I hope that you are fortunate in winning your Demetrius!

225 Keep word, Lysander; we must starve our sight
From lovers' food till morrow deep midnight.

LYSANDER
I will, my Hermia.

[*Exit* HERMIA.]

Helena, adieu;
As you on him, Demetrius dote on you!

[*Exit* LYSANDER.]

HELENA
230 How happy some o'er other some can be!
Through Athens I am thought as fair as she.
But what of that? Demetrius thinks not so;
He will not know what all but he do know.
And, as he errs, doting on Hermia's eyes,
235 So I, admiring of his qualities.
Things base and vile, holding no quantity,
Love can **transpose** to form and dignity.
Love looks not with the eyes but with the mind;
And therefore is wing'd Cupid painted blind.
240 Nor hath Love's mind of any judgment taste.
Wings and no eyes, figure unheedy haste;
And therefore is Love said to be a child,
Because in choice he is so oft beguil'd.
As waggish boys in game themselves forswear,
245 So the boy Love is perjur'd everywhere:
For ere Demetrius look'd on Hermia's eyne,
He hail'd down oaths that he was only mine;
And when this hail some heat from Hermia felt,
So he dissolv'd, and show'rs of oaths did melt.
250 I will go tell him of fair Hermia's flight;
Then to the wood will he tomorrow night
Pursue her. And, for this intelligence
If I have thanks, it is a dear expense.
But herein mean I to enrich my pain,
255 To have his sight thither and back again.

[*Exit.*]

Keep your word, Lysander. We must starve our eyes   225
of the sight of each other until tomorrow at dark midnight.

LYSANDER
I will, my Hermia.

> HERMIA *exits.*

Good-bye, Helena.
May Demetrius love you as you love him.

> LYSANDER *exits.*

HELENA
How happy some people can be in comparison to others.   230
People all over Athens think I am as beautiful as she.
But what of that? Demetrius doesn't think so.
He refuses to know what everyone except he knows.
And as he makes a mistake, adoring Hermia's eyes,
so I make a mistake, admiring all of his characteristics.   235
Things can be worthless, ugly, and unattractive,
and love can change them to beauty and dignity.
Love doesn't look with his eyes, but with his mind,
and that is why winged Cupid is pictured blind.
Love's mind doesn't have a scrap of judgment, either—   240
wings and no eyes symbolize thoughtless haste.
And, therefore, Love is said to be a child
because in making his choices, his is so often misled.
Just as playful boys in fun lie,
so the boy, Love, is perjured everywhere.   245
For before Demetrius looked in Hermia's eyes,
he hailed down vows that he loved me only.
But when his hail felt some of Hermia's heat,
he dissolved and his shower of vows melted.
I will go tell him of beautiful Hermia's flight.   250
Then to the woods tomorrow night, he will
follow her. And for this information,
if he thanks me, Demetrius will consider it a heavy cost.
But I'll be repaid for my pain
by just the sight of him going and coming back again.   255

> *Exit.*

ACT I, SCENE II

[*Athens, Quince's house.*] *Enter* QUINCE, SNUG,
BOTTOM, FLUTE, SNOUT, *and* STARVELING.

QUINCE

Is all our company here?

BOTTOM

You were best to call them generally,* man by man,
according to the scrip.

QUINCE

Here is the scroll of every man's name, which is thought
5 fit, through all Athens, to play in our interlude before the
Duke and the Duchess, on his wedding day at night.

BOTTOM

First, good Peter Quince, say what the play treats on, then
read the names of the actors, and so grow to a point.

QUINCE

Marry,* our play is "The most lamentable comedy, and
10 most cruel death of Pyramus and Thisbe."*

BOTTOM

A very good piece of work, I assure you, and a merry. Now,
good Peter Quince, call forth your actors by the scroll.
Masters, spread yourselves.

QUINCE

Answer as I call you. Nick Bottom, the weaver.

BOTTOM

15 Ready. Name what part I am for, and proceed.

QUINCE

You, Nick Bottom, are set down for Pyramus.

---

2 *generally* Bottom's malapropism (unintentionally humorous substitution of one
word for another) for "severally" or "individually"

9 *Marry* exclamation coming from the oath "by the Virgin Mary," meaning
"indeed" or "really"

10 *Pyramus and Thisbe* two Babylonian lovers. Their story is similar to Romeo and
Juliet's.

ACT 1, SCENE 2

Quince's house. QUINCE, *the carpenter;* SNUG, *the joiner;* BOTTOM, *the weaver;* FLUTE, *the bellows-mender;* SNOUT, *the tinker; and* STARVELING, *the tailor, all enter.*

QUINCE

Is all of our company here?

BOTTOM

You'd better call them generally, man by man, according to the script.

QUINCE

Here is a list of every man's name who is considered fit, throughout all of Athens, to play in our drama before the Duke   5 and Duchess, on their wedding day at night.

BOTTOM

First, good Peter Quince, tell us what the play is about, then read the names of the actors. Come to the point in that way.

QUINCE

Very well, our play is called, "The most lamentable comedy and most cruel death of Pyramus and Thisbe."   10

BOTTOM

It's a very good piece of work, I assure you, and a funny one. Now, good Peter Quince, call forward your actors from your list. Masters, spread out.

QUINCE

Answer as I call your name. Nick Bottom, the weaver.

BOTTOM

Ready. Tell me what part I have and proceed.   15

QUINCE

You, Nick Bottom, are set down to play Pyramus.

BOTTOM

What is Pyramus? A lover or a tyrant?

QUINCE

A lover that kills himself most gallant for love.

BOTTOM

20 That will ask some tears in the true performing of it. If I do it, let the audience look to their eyes. I will move storms; I will condole in some measure. To the rest.—Yet my chief humour is for a tyrant.* I could play Ercles rarely, or a part to tear a cat in, to make all split.

"The raging rocks
25 And shivering shocks
Shall break the locks
Of prison gates;
And Phibbus's* car
Shall shine from far
30 And make and mar
The foolish Fates."*

This was lofty! Now name the rest of players. This is Ercles's vein, a tyrant's vein; a lover is more condoling.

QUINCE

Francis Flute, the bellows-mender.

FLUTE

35 Here, Peter Quince.

QUINCE

Flute, you must take Thisbe on you.

FLUTE

What is Thisbe? A wand'ring knight?

---

22 *tyrant* a type of character found in medieval and Renaissance plays. A typical tyrant, such as the character Hercules, was a violent ranter.

28 *Phibbus* Bottom's malapropism for Phoebus, the sun god. The god's chariot is the sun.

31 *Fates* three goddesses who determined the fate of humans. Clotho spun the thread of each individual's fate; Lachesis decided each man's lot; and Atropos broke the thread of life.

BOTTOM

Who is Pyramus? A lover or a tyrant?

QUINCE

He is a lover who kills himself most gallantly for love.

BOTTOM

That will call for some tears in an honest performance of the part.
If I do it, let the audience watch out for their eyes! I will move   20
them to storms; I will grieve to some degree. Go on with your
list—yet my best talent is for playing a tyrant. I could play
Hercules beautifully, or any part which calls for ranting, to make all
ears split.

> The raging rocks
> And shivering shocks   25
> Will break the locks
>   Of prison gates.
> And Phibbus's car
> Will shine from afar
> And make and deface   30
>   The foolish Fates.

That was top-notch! Now name the rest of the players. That was
right in the vein of Hercules—the vein of a tyrant. A lover is more
sympathetic.

QUINCE

Francis Flute, the bellows-mender.

FLUTE

Here, Peter Quince.   35

QUINCE

Flute, you must play Thisbe.

FLUTE

Who is Thisbe? A wandering knight?

QUINCE

It is the lady that Pyramus must love.

FLUTE

Nay, faith, let not me play a woman. I have a beard
40   coming.

QUINCE

That's all one. You shall play it in a mask, and you may
speak as small as you will.

BOTTOM

An I may hide my face, let me play Thisbe too. I'll speak
in a monstrous little voice, "Thisne!* Thisne!—"Ah
45   Pyramus, my lover dear! Thy Thisbe dear, and lady dear!"

QUINCE

No, no, you must play Pyramus—and, Flute, you Thisbe.

BOTTOM

Well, proceed.

QUINCE

Robin Starveling, the tailor.

STARVELING

Here, Peter Quince.

QUINCE

50   Robin Starveling, you must play Thisbe's mother.—Tom
Snout, the tinker.*

SNOUT

Here, Peter Quince.

QUINCE

You, Pyramus's father.—Myself, Thisbe's father.—Snug the
joiner,* you, the lion's part.—And I hope here is a play
55   fitted.

---

44 *Thisne* may mean "in this way" or may be Bottom's imitation of Thisbe's high,
soft voice.

51 *tinker* a craftsman who repairs pots and pans

54 *joiner* a craftsman who does woodwork

QUINCE

She is the lady Pyramus loves.

FLUTE

No, really, don't make me play a woman. I'm growing a beard.   40

QUINCE

That makes no difference. You'll play the part in a mask, and you should speak as softly as possible.

BOTTOM

If I can hide my face in a mask, let me play Thisbe, too. I'll speak in a monstrously small voice, "Thisne, Thisne!"—"Ah, Pyramus, my dear lover! I'm your dear Thisbe, your dear lady!"   45

QUINCE

No, no! You must play Pyramus, and Flute must play Thisbe.

BOTTOM

Well, go ahead.

QUINCE

Robin Starveling, the tailor.

STARVELING

Here, Peter Quince.

QUINCE

Robin Starveling, you must play Thisbe's mother. Tom Snout,   50
the tinker.

SNOUT

Here, Peter Quince.

QUINCE

You will play Pyramus's father. I will play Thisbe's father. Snug, the joiner, you will play the lion's part. I hope we have a well-cast play.   55

SNUG

Have you the lion's part written? Pray you, if it be, give it me, for I am slow of study.

QUINCE

You may do it extempore, for it is nothing but roaring.

BOTTOM

60　Let me play the lion too. I will roar that I will do any man's heart good to hear me. I will roar that I will make the Duke say, "Let him roar again. Let him roar again!"

QUINCE

An you should do it too terribly, you would fright the Duchess and the ladies that they would shriek; and that were enough to hang us all.

ALL

65　That would hang us, every mother's son.

BOTTOM

I grant you, friends, if you should fright the ladies out of their wits, they would have no more **discretion** but to hang us. But I will aggravate* my voice so that I will roar you as gently as any sucking dove.* I will roar you an 70　'twere any nightingale.

QUINCE

You can play no part but Pyramus, for Pyramus is a sweet-fac'd man, a proper man as one shall see in a summer's day, a most lovely gentlemanlike man. Therefore you must needs play Pyramus.

BOTTOM

75　Well, I will undertake it. What beard were I best to play it in?

QUINCE

Why, what you will.

BOTTOM

I will discharge it in either your straw-colour beard, your orange-tawny beard, your purple-in-grain beard, or your French-crown-colour beard, your perfit yellow.

68　*aggravate* Bottom really means "moderate."

69　*sucking dove* Bottom confuses "sucking" (not weaned) with "sitting" (hatching).

SNUG

Have you written down the lion's part? I beg you, if you have, give it to me, for I'm a slow study.

QUINCE

You may do it extemporaneously, for it's nothing but roaring.

BOTTOM

Let me play the lion, too. I will roar so that it will do any man's heart good to hear me. I will roar so that I will make the Duke say, 60 "Let him roar again, let him roar again!"

QUINCE

If you did it too frighteningly, you would scare the Duchess and the ladies so that they would scream, and that'd be enough to hang us all.

ALL

That would hang us, every mother's son of us. 65

BOTTOM

I'll admit, friends, that if the ladies would be frightened out of their wits, they would have no more sense than to hang us, but I will aggravate my voice so that I will roar as gently as any sucking dove. I will roar as if I were a nightingale. 70

QUINCE

You can play no part except Pyramus, for Pyramus is a sweet-faced man, as handsome a man as one shall see in a summer's day, a most lovely, gentlemanlike man. Therefore, you must play Pyramus.

BOTTOM

Well, I'll act the part. Which beard would it be best to play it in? 75

QUINCE

Why, do you whatever you like.

BOTTOM

I will play the part in either your straw-colored beard, your orange-tawny beard, your permanently dyed purple beard, or your French gold-coin-colored beard—your perfect golden.

QUINCE

80   Some of your French crowns* have no hair* at all, and
then you will play barefac'd. But, masters, here are your
parts; and I am to entreat you, request you, and desire
you, to con them by tomorrow night and meet me in the
palace wood, a mile without the town, by moonlight.
85   There will we rehearse, for if we meet in the city, we shall
be dogg'd with company and our devices known. In the
meantime I will draw a bill of properties such as our play
wants. I pray you, fail me not.

BOTTOM

    We will meet, and there we may rehearse most obscenely*
90   and courageously. Take pains. Be perfit. Adieu.

QUINCE

    At the Duke's oak we meet.

BOTTOM

    Enough. Hold or cut bow-strings.

        [*Exeunt.*]

---

80   *crown* means both "French coin" and "head"

80   *Some . . . hair* Syphilis, which caused baldness, was supposed to be very
common among the French.

89   *obscenely* another malapropism. Bottom probably means "in private."

QUINCE

Some of your French crowns have no hair at all, so you would   80
have to play it barefaced. But, gentlemen, here are your parts.
(*Hands out parts.*) I beg you, request you, and desire you to study
them by tomorrow night. And meet in the palace woods, a mile
outside of town, by moonlight. There we'll rehearse because   85
if we meet in the city, we will be dogged by onlookers and our
plans will be known. In the meantime, I will draw up a list of
props that we need for our play. I beg you, don't fail me.

BOTTOM

We will meet, and there we'll rehearse most obscenely and
courageously. Study hard, be word-perfect. Good-bye.   90

QUINCE

We'll meet at the Duke's oak.

BOTTOM

Good enough. Keep your word, or give up your parts.

> *They exit.*

Act I Review

Discussion Questions

1. Egeus insists that his daughter Hermia must marry Demetrius. If she refuses, she must either become a nun or be put to death. How much influence do you think parents should have over whom their sons or daughters marry?

2. In the first scene, Hermia complains that the more she hates Demetrius, the man her father wants her to marry, the more he follows her. Why do you think some people persist in romance despite rejection?

3. In Shakespeare's day, male actors performed the roles of women. In the play within the play, the effect is comical when Flute takes on the role of Thisbe. Reread the passage in Scene ii in which Flute is assigned his role (lines 36–42), and consider some comedies you've seen in which men dress as women. Why do you think this technique often continues to succeed in modern comedies?

4. Identify the characters that have so far experienced jealousy. How does jealousy motivate them to act?

5. What are some of the unpleasant aspects of love revealed in Act I?

Literary Elements

1. At the end of Scene i, Helena has a **soliloquy**, or a long speech in which only the audience hears the character's thoughts and feelings. What do you think her soliloquy accomplishes?

2. **Repetition** is one of Shakespeare's favorite means of poetic expression, which he uses to stress the importance of an idea or detail. Find an example of repetition in Act I, and explain what you think its effect is.

3. Bottom is fond of **oxymorons**, or linked words that contradict each other, such as "loving hate." Find an example of one of his oxymorons in Act I. What do you think it contributes to the comedy?

4. What is implied by the **title** of the play within the play: "The most lamentable comedy, and most cruel death of Pyramus and Thisbe?"

Writing Prompts

1. Some people have trouble telling apart the two young women (Hermia and Helena) and two young men (Lysander and Demetrius) in this play. Pretend you are a casting director. Cast current actors in these four roles, striving for contrast. Write a paragraph for each actor/role that explains the reasons for your choices.

2. Do a modern adaptation of Act I, Scene i. Update the language, situations, and reactions. Make it more contemporary and informal than the modern translation.

3. Write a soliloquy in Shakespeare's language, giving Hermia's reaction to one of the alternatives given her by Theseus: (a) marry Demetrius; (b) take a vow to remain unmarried and go to a convent; or (c) be put to death.

4. Imagine you have just been cast in a play and one of your fellow actors is Nick Bottom. Describe him in an email to a friend.

5. Some famous lines from Act I include "I would my father look'd but with my eyes"; "The course of true love never did run smooth"; "So quick bright things come to confusion"; and "I am slow of study." Rewrite each quotation in your own words and discuss why you think it is still remembered and quoted.

A Midsummer Night's Dream

ACT II

A Brazilian setting is used for this 1987 performance at the Public Theater, New York

"Ill met by moonlight,
proud Titania."

Before You Read

1. Sigmund Freud, often described as the father of modern psychology, once said, "You are always insane when you are in love." Explain whether you agree and why.

2. How do you think the friendship of Hermia and Helena will be affected by the fact that Helena has tipped Demetrius off about Hermia's secret plan to meet Lysander in the woods? Explain.

3. The Elizabethans viewed Midsummer's Day as a period of madness, when fairies were everywhere and magic was powerful. In what ways do you think the forest setting in Act II might work better for magic tricks and fairy characters than the city?

4. Do you agree with the saying, "All is fair in love and war"? Explain your answer.

Literary Elements

1. **Exposition** is information that is directly conveyed or explained; it gives facts necessary to understanding the play. In Act I, in her soliloquy, Helena explains that she is going to tell Demetrius about the secret plan to meet in the woods.

2. The overall atmosphere or feeling of a piece of writing is its **mood**. The mood in Act I, Scene ii, when the workmen are rehearsing, is silly and playful.

3. The difference between what is expected and what actually happens is one form of **irony**. It is ironic that Theseus wooed Hippolyta with his sword and won her love by injuring her. Usually such acts would result in hate, not love.

Words to Know

The following vocabulary words appear in Act II in the original text of Shakespeare's play. However, they are words that are still used today. Read the definitions here and pay attention to the words as you read the play (they will be in boldfaced type).

beguile	charm; enchant
dissembling	lying; deceptive
dissension	disagreement; argument
impeach	cast doubt upon; accuse
languish	long for; pine
progeny	children; offspring
sentinel	guard; watch
surfeit	overabundunce; excess
valor [valour]	bravery; courage
wanton	wild; untamed

Act Summary

A group of fairies have come to celebrate the Duke's wedding and are gathered to frolic in the woods. Their prime mischief-maker is Puck, also known as Robin Goodfellow, who is servant to Oberon, King of the Fairies. Oberon is jealous of the Athenian duke, Theseus, because his wife, Titania, once loved him. He is also disgruntled with Titania because both want to have the same boy—whom they have taken from his home in India—as an attendant. To retaliate, Oberon asks Puck to drop a magic potion into Titania's eyes, one that will make her fall in love with the first creature she sees upon awakening.

Acting on Helena's tip, Demetrius has come into the woods to pursue Lysander and Hermia, with Helena following. Oberon, who sympathizes with the lovesick Helena because Demetrius scorns her, orders Puck to drop a magic potion into the eyes of Demetrius as well. Instead, a careless Puck drops the potion into the eyes of the sleeping Lysander, who is lying near Hermia, also asleep. When Lysander awakens, the first person he sees is Helena. The magic works so well that he leaves Hermia's side and pursues Helena, who is convinced he is still in love with her friend and cruelly making fun of her.

Dominic West as Lysander and Calista Flockhart as Helena, 1999 film of the play

ACT II, SCENE I

[*A wood near Athens.*] *Enter a* FAIRY *at one door and*
ROBIN GOODFELLOW *at another.*

ROBIN GOODFELLOW
How now, spirit! Whither wander you?

FAIRY
"Over hill, over dale,
    Thorough bush, thorough brier,
Over park, over pale,
    Thorough flood, thorough fire,
5   I do wander everywhere,
Swifter than the moon's sphere.
And I serve the Fairy Queen,
To dew her orbs upon the green.
10   The cowslips tall her pensioners* be;
In their gold coats spots you see;
Those be rubies, fairy favours,
In those freckles live their savours."
I must go seek some dewdrops here
15   And hang a pearl in every cowslip's ear.
Farewell, thou lob of spirits; I'll be gone.
Our Queen and all her elves come here anon.

ROBIN GOODFELLOW
The King doth keep his revels here tonight;
Take heed the Queen come not within his sight;
20   For Oberon is passing fell and wrath,
Because that, she as her attendant, hath
A lovely boy stolen from an Indian king.
She never had so sweet a changeling.*
And jealous Oberon would have the child
25   Knight of his train, to trace the forests wild.
But she perforce withholds the loved boy,
Crowns him with flowers, and makes him all her joy.

---

10 *pensioners* Queen Elizabeth I's fifty noble bodyguards were called gentlemen
pensioners.

23 *changeling* a child stolen by the fairies or the child they leave in the place of the
kidnapped victim

ACT 2, SCENE 1

A woods near Athens. A FAIRY enters at one entrance and
ROBIN GOODFELLOW (PUCK), *at another.*

PUCK

Well, spirit, where are you wandering to?

FAIRY

> *Over hill, over dale,*
> > *Through bushes, through briers,*
> *Over park, over land,*
> > *Through flood, through fire;* 5
> *I wander everywhere*
> *Swifter than the moon revolves.*
> *I serve the Fairy Queen,*
> *Putting dew on her fairy rings on the green.*
> *The tall cowslips are her guards.* 10
> *You can see spots on their gold coats,*
> *Which are rubies, fairy gifts—*
> *In those freckles live their perfumes.*

I must go find some dewdrops here,
And hang a pearl in every cowslip's ear. 15
Good-bye, you clumsy lout of spirits. I'll go.
Our Queen and all her elves will be here soon.

PUCK

King Oberon will hold his festivities here tonight.
Make sure the Queen does not come near him
because Oberon is very enraged and angry 20
because she has taken for her attendant
a lovely boy whom she stole from an Indian king.
She never had such a sweet changeling.
Jealous Oberon wants the child to be
a knight in his train of followers, who roam the wild forests. 25
But she withholds the beloved boy by force,
crowning him with flowers, and takes all her joy in him.

And now they never meet in a grove or green,
By fountain clear, or spangled starlight sheen,
30 But they do square, that all their elves for fear
Creep into acorn cups and hide them there.

FAIRY

Either I mistake your shape and making quite,
Or else you are that shrewd and knavish sprite
Call'd Robin Goodfellow. Are not you he
35 That frights the maidens of the villagery,
Skim milk, and sometimes labour in the quern
And bootless make the breathless housewife churn,
And sometime make the drink to bear no barm,
Mislead night wanderers, laughing at their harm?
40 Those that "Hobgoblin" call you, and "sweet Puck,"
You do their work, and they shall have good luck.
Are not you he?

ROBIN GOODFELLOW
Thou speakest aright,
I am that merry wanderer of the night.
45 I jest to Oberon and make him smile
When I a fat and bean-fed horse **beguile,**
Neighing in likeness of a filly foal.
And sometime lurk I in a gossip's bowl
In very likeness of a roasted crab,*
50 And, when she drinks, against her lips I bob
And on her withered dewlap pour the ale.
The wisest aunt, telling the saddest tale,
Sometime for three-foot stool mistaketh me;
Then slip I from her bum, down topples she,
55 And "Tailor!" cries, and falls into a cough;
And then the whole quire hold their hips and loffe
And waxen in their mirth and neeze and swear
A merrier hour was never wasted there.
But, room, fairy! Here comes Oberon.

---

49 *crab* or crabapple, frequently added to punches

And now they never meet in grove or green,
by clear fountain, or bright, shining starlight,
that they don't quarrel so that all their elves, out of fear,   30
crawl into acorn cups and hide there.

FAIRY

Either I mistake your shape and looks,
or you are that impish and mischievous elf
called Robin Goodfellow. Aren't you the one
Who frightens the girls of the village folk,   35
skims the milk, and sometimes clogs the grain grinder?
Aren't you the one who makes the breathless housewife churn for
    butter in vain?
And sometimes don't you make beer without yeast?
Don't you mislead night wanderers and laugh at the scrapes they
    get into?
For those who call you Hobgoblin and sweet Puck,   40
you do their work, and they have good luck.
Aren't you the one?

PUCK

You are right.
I am that merry nighttime wanderer.
I make jokes for Oberon. I make him smile,   45
when I charm a fat and bean-fed horse
by neighing like a young filly.
and sometimes I lurk in an old woman's hot punch,
looking just like a roasted crab apple.
Then when she drinks, I bob against her lips,   50
and I pour ale on the withered skin of her throat.
The wisest old woman, telling the most serious story,
sometimes thinks I'm a three-foot stool.
Then I slip out from under her bum and she falls down,
and she cries "Tailor" and starts to cough.   55
Then the whole group hold their hips and laugh,
and become merrier and sneeze and swear they
have never passed a happier hour there.
But, make way, fairy! Here comes Oberon.

FAIRY

60   And here my mistress. Would that he were gone!

> Enter OBERON, *the King of Fairies, at one door with his*
> TRAIN; *and* TITANIA, *the Queen, at another with hers.*

OBERON

Ill met by moonlight, proud Titania.

TITANIA

What, jealous Oberon! Fairies, skip hence.
I have forsworn his bed and company.

OBERON

Tarry, rash wanton! Am not I thy lord?

TITANIA

65   Then I must be thy lady. But I know
When thou hast stolen away from Fairyland
And in the shape of Corin sat all day,
Playing on pipes of corn and versing love
To amorous Phillida.* Why art thou here,
70   Come from the farthest steep of India?
But that, forsooth, the bouncing Amazon,
Your buskin'd* mistress and your warrior love,
To Theseus must be wedded, and you come
To give their bed joy and prosperity.

OBERON

75   How canst thou thus for shame, Titania,
Glance at my credit with Hippolyta,
Knowing I know thy love to Theseus?
Didst thou not lead him through the glimmering night
From Perigenia, whom he ravished?
80   And made him with fair Aegles break his faith,
With Ariadne and Antiopa?*

TITANIA

These are the forgeries of jealousy;

67–69   *Corin . . . Phillida* commonplace names for a lover in pastoral poetry

72   *buskin'd* wearing high boots

79–81   *Perigenia . . . Antiopa* Theseus's deserted lovers

FAIRY

And here comes my mistress. I wish he were gone.   60

> OBERON, *the King of Fairies, enters at one door with his* TRAIN
> *and* TITANIA, *the Queen, enters at another with hers.*

OBERON

This is an unwelcome meeting by moonlight, proud Titania.

TITANIA

So! Jealous Oberon! Fairies, let's skip away.
I have vowed to avoid his bed and his company.

OBERON

Wait, rash, undisciplined woman! Am I not your lord?

TITANIA

Then I must be your lady. But I know   65
that you have skipped away from fairyland
and disguised as Corin sat all day
playing on grain stalk pipes and spouting love poetry
to the amorous Phillida. Why did you come here
from the most remote plain of India,   70
unless, of course, the swaggering Amazon,
your booted mistress and your warrior lover,
is going to be married to Theseus and you have come
to wish the couple joy and prosperity?

OBERON

For shame, Titania.   75
How can you slander my reputation with talk about Hippolyta,
when you know I know of your love for Theseus?
Didn't you lead him through the glimmering night
from Perigenia, whom he raped?
And then you made him break his promise to the lovely Aegles   80
and Ariadne and Antiopa?

TITANIA

Those are lies of jealousy.

And never, since the middle summer's spring,
Met we on hill, in dale, forest or mead,
85   By paved fountain or by rushy brook,
Or in the beached margent of the sea,
To dance our ringlets to the whistling wind,
But with thy brawls thou hast disturb'd our sport.
Therefore the winds, piping to us in vain,
90   As in revenge have suck'd up from the sea
Contagious fogs, which, falling in the land,
Hath every pelting river made so proud
That they have overborne their continents.
The ox hath therefore stretch'd his yoke in vain,
95   The ploughman lost his sweat, and the green corn
Hath rotted ere his youth attain'd a beard.
The fold stands empty in the drowned field,
And crows are fatted with the murrain flock.
The nine-men's-morris* is fill'd up with mud,
100   And the quaint mazes in the wanton green,
For lack of tread, are undistinguishable.
The human mortals want their winter here.
No night is now with hymn or carol blest.
Therefore the moon, the governess of floods,
105   Pale in her anger, washes all the air,
That rheumatic diseases do abound.
And thorough this distemperature we see
The seasons alter: hoary-headed frosts
Fall in the fresh lap of the crimson rose,
110   And on old Hiems's* thin and icy crown
An odorous chaplet of sweet summer buds
Is, as in mockery, set; the spring, the summer,
The childing autumn, angry winter, change
Their wonted liveries; and the mazed world,
115   By their increase, now knows not which is which.
And this same **progeny** of evils comes
From our debate, from our **dissension;**
We are the parents and original.

---

99   *nine-men's-morris* the squares created on a lawn for a checker-like game

110   *Hiem* the personification of winter

Never, since the beginning of midsummer,
have we met on hill, in dale, forest, or meadow,
by pebble-bottomed fountain or by rush-lined brook,   85
or along the seashore,
to dance our circling steps in the whistling wind,
that you haven't disturbed our pleasure with your storms.
Therefore the winds whistle to us in vain,
as if out of revenge, having sucked up from the sea   90
fogs that carry disease, which, rolling inland,
have made every little river so proud
that they have overflowed their banks.
Therefore the ox has pulled the plough in vain,
the plowman has wasted his sweat, and the green grain   95
has rotted before it could mature.
The pens stand empty in the drowned field,
and crows have grown fat on the dead diseased cattle.
The morris game field is full of mud,
and intricate paths through the deep grass   100
have faded for lack of use.
The human mortals lack their winter here.
But no night is now made merry with a hymn or carol.
Therefore, the moon, the ruler of floods,
pale in her anger, washes all the air,   105
which is full of rheumatic diseases.
Through this disturbance in nature, we see
the seasons have been mixed up. White frosts
fall in the fresh lap of the crimson rose.
On old winter's thin and icy head,   110
a fragrant wreath of sweet summer buds
is placed in mockery. The spring, the summer,
the fruitful autumn, and angry winter change
their usual clothes, and the confused world
cannot tell which is which from nature's signs.   115
These very children of evil come
from our quarrel and from our argument.
We are their parents and origin.

OBERON

Do you amend it then. It lies in you.
120 Why should Titania cross her Oberon?
I do but beg a little changeling boy
To be my henchman.

TITANIA

Set your heart at rest:
The Fairyland buys not the child of me.
125 His mother was a vot'ress of my order,
And, in the spiced Indian air, by night,
Full often hath she gossip'd by my side
And sat with me on Neptune's* yellow sands,
Marking th' embarked traders on the flood,
130 When we have laugh'd to see the sails conceive
And grow big-bellied with the **wanton** wind;
Which she with pretty and with swimming gait,
Following—her womb then rich with my young squire—
Would imitate and sail upon the land
135 To fetch me trifles and return again,
As from a voyage, rich with merchandise.
But she, being mortal, of that boy did die;
And for her sake do I rear up her boy,
And for her sake I will not part with him.

OBERON

140 How long within this wood intend you stay?

TITANIA

Perchance till after Theseus's wedding day.
If you will patiently dance in our round
And see our moonlight revels, go with us.
If not, shun me, and I will spare your haunts.

OBERON

145 Give me that boy, and I will go with thee.

TITANIA

Not for thy fairy kingdom. Fairies, away!
We shall chide downright if I longer stay.

---

128   *Neptune* the god who ruled the ocean

OBERON

You had better correct it, then. It is up to you.
Why should Titania thwart her Oberon? 120
All I ask for is a little changeling boy
to be my page.

TITANIA

Set your heart at rest.
You could not buy him from me if you offered your entire
fairyland.
His mother was a woman who took a vow to worship me. 125
And in the spiced Indian air, at night,
she often chatted by my side
and sat with me on the sea's yellow sands.
We watched the sailing traders on the sea
and laughed to see the sails conceive 130
and grow fat with the playful winds.
She, with a pretty and graceful walk—
her womb then was filled with my young page—
would imitate the ship and sail across the land
to fetch me little things and return again— 135
as if from a voyage—rich with merchandise.
But she, being just a mortal, died delivering the boy.
For her sake, I raise her boy,
and for her sake, I will not part with him.

OBERON

How long do you intend to stay in these woods? 140

TITANIA

Perhaps until after Theseus's wedding day.
If you will patiently join in our circular dance
and see our moonlight festivities, come with us.
If not, avoid me, and I will keep away from you.

OBERON

Give me that boy, and I'll go with you. 145

TITANIA

Not for your fairy kingdom. Fairies, let's be off!
We will quarrel outright if I stay any longer.

[*Exit* TITANIA *with her* TRAIN.]

OBERON

Well, go thy way. Thou shalt not from this grove
Till I torment thee for this injury.—

150 My gentle Puck, come hither. Thou rememb'rest
Since once I sat upon a promontory
And heard a mermaid on a dolphin's back
Uttering such dulcet and harmonious breath
That the rude sea grew civil at her song

155 And certain stars shot madly from their spheres,
To hear the sea-maid's music?

ROBIN GOODFELLOW

                    I remember.

OBERON

That very time I saw, but thou couldst not,
Flying between the cold moon and the earth,

160 Cupid all arm'd. A certain aim he took
At a fair vestal* throned by the west,
And loos'd his love-shaft smartly from his bow
As it should pierce a hundred thousand hearts;
But I might see young Cupid's fiery shaft

165 Quench'd in the chaste beams of the wat'ry room,
And the imperial vot'ress passed on
In maiden meditation, fancy-free.
Yet mark'd I where the bolt of Cupid fell.
It fell upon a little western flower,

170 Before, milk-white, now purple with love's wound,
And maidens call it "love-in-idleness."*
Fetch me that flower, the herb I shew'd thee once.
The juice of it on sleeping eyelids laid
Will make or man or woman madly dote

175 Upon the next live creature that it sees.
Fetch me this herb, and be thou here again
Ere the leviathan can swim a league.

---

161   *vestal* usually considered to be a reference to Queen Elizabeth I. (The queen may
have been present when *A Midsummer Night's Dream* was first performed.)

171   *love-in-idleness* another name for the flower, the pansy

TITANIA *and her* TRAIN *exit.*

OBERON
Well, go on your way. But, you will not leave this woods
until I punish you for this insult.
My gentle Puck, come here. You remember   150
the time I once sat on a promontory
and heard a mermaid, on a dolphin's back,
singing such sweet and harmonious notes
that the rude sea grew well-behaved when she sang,
and some stars shot madly out of their orbits   155
to hear the sea maiden's music.

PUCK
I remember.

OBERON
On that particular occasion I saw, but you could not,
flying between the cold moon and the earth,
Cupid, all armed with arrows. He took aim   160
at a lovely virgin enthroned by the west,
and he shot his love arrow briskly from his bow,
as if he meant it to pierce a hundred thousand hearts.
But I could see young Cupid's fiery arrow
quenched in the pure beams of the watery moon,   165
and the regal worshipper passed on
in virginal meditation, free from the influence of love.
Yet I saw where Cupid's arrow fell.
It fell upon a little western flower,
that was once milk-white and now is purple from love's wound. 170
Girls call it "love-in-idleness."
Bring me that flower; I showed it to you once.
If the juice of it is dropped on sleeping eyelids,
it will make either man or woman adore
the next creature he or she sees.   175
Bring me this flower, and be back again
before the whale can swim three miles.

ROBIN GOODFELLOW

I'll put a girdle round about the earth
In forty minutes.

[*Exit.*]

OBERON

180   Having once this juice,
I'll watch Titania when she is asleep
And drop the liquor of it in her eyes.
The next thing then she waking, looks upon,
Be it on lion, bear, or wolf, or bull,
185   On meddling monkey, or on busy ape,
She shall pursue it with the soul of love.
And ere I take this charm from off her sight,
As I can take it with another herb,
I'll make her render up her page to me.
190   But who comes here? I am invisible,
And I will overhear their conference.

     Enter DEMETRIUS, HELENA *following him.*

DEMETRIUS

I love thee not, therefore pursue me not.
Where is Lysander and fair Hermia?
The one I'll stay; the other stayeth me.
195   Thou told'st me they were stol'n unto this wood,
And here am I, and wood within this wood
Because I cannot meet my Hermia.
Hence, get thee gone, and follow me no more.

HELENA

You draw me, you hard-hearted adamant!*
200   But yet you draw not iron,* for my heart
Is true as steel. Leave you your power to draw,
And I shall have no power to follow you.

DEMETRIUS

Do I entice you? Do I speak you fair?
Or, rather, do I not in plainest truth
205   Tell you, I do not nor I cannot love you?

---

199   *adamant* means both a magnet and a type of very hard metal

200   *iron* another hard metal, implying he is unfeeling and cold

PUCK
> I'll fly around the earth
> in forty minutes.

> *He exits.*

OBERON
> Once I have this juice,   180
> I'll wait until Titania is asleep
> and drop this juice in her eyes.
> When she awakes, the first thing she looks at,
> whether it be a lion, a bear, a wolf, a bull,
> a meddling monkey, or an annoying ape,   185
> she will pursue it with all her love.
> And before I lift this magical charm from her vision,
> which I can remove with another herb,
> I'll make her give up her page to me.
> But who is coming? Since I'm invisible,   190
> I will listen to their conversation.

> DEMETRIUS *enters with* HELENA *following him.*

DEMETRIUS
> I don't love you, so stop following me.
> Where is Lysander and the lovely Hermia?
> One of them I'd like to kill; the other one is killing me.
> You told me that they had sneaked off into this woods.   195
> And here I am, out of my mind within this woods
> because I cannot find my Hermia.
> Go, be off, and don't follow me anymore!

HELENA
> You draw me to you, you hard-hearted magnet.
> But you are not attracting iron because my heart   200
> is as true as steel. Give up your power to attract,
> and I will not have the power to follow you.

DEMETRIUS
> Do I entice you? Do I speak to you kindly?
> Or, rather, don't I tell you as bluntly as possible
> that I do not and cannot love you?   205

HELENA

And even for that do I love you the more.
I am your spaniel, and, Demetrius,
The more you beat me, I will fawn on you.
Use me but as your spaniel: spurn me, strike me,
210 Neglect me, lose me; only give me leave,
Unworthy as I am, to follow you.
What worser place can I beg in your love—
And yet a place of high respect with me—
Than to be used as you use your dog?

DEMETRIUS

215 Tempt not too much the hatred of my spirit,
For I am sick when I do look on thee.

HELENA

And I am sick when I look not on you.

DEMETRIUS

You do **impeach** your modesty too much
To leave the city and commit yourself
220 Into the hands of one that loves you not,
To trust the opportunity of night
And the ill counsel of a desert place
With the rich worth of your virginity.

HELENA

Your virtue is my privilege. For that
225 Is not night when I do see your face,
Therefore I think I am not in the night.
Nor doth this wood lack worlds of company,
For you, in my respect, are all the world.
Then how can it be said I am alone
230 When all the world is here to look on me?

DEMETRIUS

I'll run from thee and hide me in the brakes,
And leave thee to the mercy of wild beasts.

HELENA

The wildest hath not such a heart as you.
Run when you will, the story shall be chang'd:

HELENA

And even for that very reason I love you all the more.
I am your spaniel, and, Demetrius,
the more you beat me, the more I will fawn on you.
Treat me just like your spaniel—reject me, hit me,
neglect me, lose me—only, give me permission,   210
unworthy as I am, to follow you.
What lower place can I beg for in your love—
and yet it would be a wonderful place to me—
than to be treated as you would your dog?

DEMETRIUS

Don't tempt my hatred too much,   215
because I grow sick whenever I see you.

HELENA

And I grow sick whenever I cannot see you.

DEMETRIUS

You're damaging your reputation too much
by leaving the city and putting yourself
into the hands of someone who doesn't love you.   220
You are trusting the dangerous possibilities of night
and the risky seclusion of a deserted place
with the rich value of your virtue.

HELENA

Your powerful appeal allows me to do so. Since
it is never night when I see your face,   225
I never think it is night.
Nor is this woods lacking for plenty of company,
because you, in my opinion, are the entire world.
So how can it be said I am alone
when all the world is here to see me?   230

DEMETRIUS

I'll run from you and hide in the thickets,
and leave you to the mercy of the wild animals.

HELENA

The wildest beast doesn't have a heart like yours.
Run when you wish—I'll change the old story:

235 Apollo flies and Daphne* holds the chase;
The dove pursues the griffin;* the mild hind
Makes speed to catch the tiger. Bootless speed
When cowardice pursues and **valour** flies.

DEMETRIUS
I will not stay thy questions. Let me go,
240 Or if thou follow me, do not believe
But I shall do thee mischief in the wood.

HELENA
Ay, in the temple, in the town, the field,
You do me mischief. Fie, Demetrius!
Your wrongs do set a scandal on my sex.
245 We cannot fight for love, as men may do.
We should be woo'd and were not made to woo.

[*Exit* DEMETRIUS.]

I'll follow thee and make a heaven of hell,
To die upon the hand I love so well.

[*Exit.*]

OBERON
Fare thee well, nymph. Ere he do leave this grove,
250 Thou shalt fly him, and he shall seek thy love.

Enter ROBIN GOODFELLOW.

Has thou the flower there? Welcome, wanderer.

ROBIN GOODFELLOW
Ay, there it is.

OBERON
I pray thee, give it me. [ROBIN *gives him
the flower.*]
I know a bank where the wild thyme blows,
255 Where oxlips and the nodding violet grows,
Quite over-canopi'd with luscious woodbine,

---

235 *Apollo . . . Daphne* The Greek god Apollo chased the nymph Daphne until she turned into a tree.

236 *griffin* a mythical beast with a lion's body and the head, wings, and front feet of a bird

Apollo runs, and Daphne chases him;   235
the dove pursues the griffin; the gentle doe
hurries to catch the tiger—useless speed
when a coward chases and the brave runs!

DEMETRIUS

I won't wait to listen to you. Let me go!
If you follow me, believe me,   240
I'll see that you come to some harm in the woods.

HELENA

Yes, in the temple, in the town, in the field,
you hurt me. Shame on you, Demetrius!
The wrongs you have done to me have made a scandal of my
     womanhood.
Women cannot fight for love as men may do.   245
Women have to be pursued. We were not made to pursue.

> DEMETRIUS *exits.*

I'll follow you and make a heaven out of hell.
I'll die by your hand which I love so well.

> *She exits.*

OBERON

Good-bye, nymph. Before he leaves this wood,
you shall run from him, and he will seek your love.   250

> PUCK *enters.*

Do you have the flower there? Welcome wanderer.

PUCK

Yes, there it is.

OBERON

Please give it to me. (PUCK *gives him the flower.*)
I know a bank where the wild thyme blows,
where oxlips and the nodding violet grows,   255
all covered with luscious woodbine,

With sweet musk-roses and with eglantine.
There sleeps Titania sometime of the night,
Lull'd in these flowers with dances and delight.
260 And there the snake throws her enamell'd skin,
Weed wide enough to wrap a fairy in.
And with the juice of this I'll streak her eyes
And make her full of hateful fantasies.
Take thou some of it, and seek through this grove.

[*He gives* ROBIN *part of the flower.*]

265 A sweet Athenian lady is in love
With a disdainful youth. Anoint his eyes,
But do it when the next thing he espies
May be the lady. Thou shalt know the man
By the Athenian garments he hath on.
270 Effect it with some care, that he may prove
More fond on her than she upon her love.
And look thou meet me ere the first cock crow.

ROBIN GOODFELLOW
Fear not, my lord, your servant shall do so.

[*Exeunt.*]

sweet musk roses, and eglantine.
Sometime Titania sleeps there at night,
lulled to sleep in these flowers with wonderful dances.
And there the snake sheds her enameled skin,   260
a garment wide enough to wrap a fairy in.
And with the juice of this flower, I'll streak her eyes,
and fill her full of hateful delusions.
Take some of this juice, and look through these woods.
A sweet Athenian lady is in love   265
with a scornful youth. Pour the flower juice in his eyes,
but do it so that the next thing he sees
will be this lady. You will recognize the man
by the Athenian clothes he has on.
Be sure to do this carefully so that he will become   270
more foolishly in love with her than she is with him.
And be sure to meet me before the first rooster crows.

PUCK
Don't worry, my lord, I will do so.

    They exit.

ACT II, SCENE II

[*Another part of the wood.*] *Enter* TITANIA, *with her* TRAIN.

TITANIA

Come, now a roundel and a fairy song;
Then, for the third part of a minute, hence—
Some to kill cankers in the muskrose buds,
Some war with reremice for their leathern wings
5   To make my small elves coats, and some keep back
The clamorous owl that nightly hoots and wonders
At our quaint spirits. Sing me now asleep.
Then to your offices and let me rest.

[*The* FAIRIES *sing.*]

1. FAIRY

"You spotted snakes with double tongue,
10   Thorny hedgehogs, be not seen.
Newts and blind-worms, do no wrong,
            Come not near our Fairy Queen."

CHORUS

"Philomel,* with melody
Sing in our sweet lullaby,
15   Lulla, lulla, lullaby, lulla, lulla, lullaby.
            Never harm
            Nor spell nor charm
Come our lovely lady nigh.
So, good night, with lullaby."

1. FAIRY

20   "Weaving spiders, come not here.
            Hence, you long-legg'd spinners, hence!
Beatles black, approach not near.
            Worm nor snail, do no offence."

CHORUS

"Philomel, with melody," etc.

---

13   *Philomel* a Greek girl who was changed into a nightingale

ACT 2, SCENE 2

Another part of the woods. TITANIA *enters with her* FOLLOWERS.

TITANIA

Come! Now dance in a ring and sing a fairy song.
Then for a third of a minute, leave here.
Some of you shall go to kill cankerworms in the musk rose buds,
some to fight bats for their leather wings
to make coats for my small elves, and some to chase away   5
the noisy owl that nightly hoots and wonders
at our dainty spirits. Sing me to sleep now.
Then do your duties, and let me sleep.

(The FAIRIES *sing.)*

FIRST FAIRY

You spotted snakes with double tongues,
　　And thorny hedgehogs, stay away.   10
Newts and little snakes, do no wrong.
　　Don't come near our fairy queen.

CHORUS

Philomel, with melody
Join our sweet lullaby.
Lulla, lulla, lullaby, lulla, lulla, lullaby,   15
　　No harm
　　Or spell, or charm,
Must come near our lovely lady.
So, good night, with lullaby.

FIRST FAIRY

Weaving spiders, don't come here.   20
　　Away, you long-legged spinners of webs, away!
Black beetles, do not approach.
　　Worms and snails, do no harm.

CHORUS

Philomel, with melody . . .   (Repeat chorus.)

2. FAIRY

25 Hence, away! Now all is well.
One aloof stand **sentinel**.

[*Exeunt* FAIRIES. TITANIA *sleeps.*]

Enter OBERON [*who squeezes the nectar on* TITANIA's *eyelids.*]

OBERON

What thou seest when thou dost wake,
Do it for thy true love take,
Love and **languish** for his sake.
30 Be it ounce, or cat, or bear,
Pard, or boar with bristled hair,
In thy eye that shall appear
When thou wak'st, it is thy dear.
Wake when some vile thing is near.

[*Exit.*]

Enter LYSANDER *and* HERMIA.

LYSANDER

35 Fair love, you faint with wand'ring in the wood;
And to speak troth, I have forgot our way.
We'll rest us, Hermia, if you think it good,
And tarry for the comfort of the day.

HERMIA

Be it so, Lysander. Find you out a bed,
40 For I upon this bank will rest my head.

LYSANDER

One turf shall serve as pillow for us both;
One heart, one bed, two bosoms and one troth.

HERMIA

Nay, good Lysander. For my sake, my dear,
Lie further off yet. Do not lie so near.

LYSANDER

45 O, take the sense, sweet, of my innocence!
Love takes the meaning in love's conference.
I mean that my heart unto yours is knit
So that but one heart we can make of it;

SECOND FAIRY

Away, away! Now all is well. 25
One of you keep watch over her from a distance.

The FAIRIES *exit.* TITANIA *sleeps.*

OBERON *enters and squeezes the flower's nectar on* TITANIA'S
eyelids.

OBERON

The first thing you see when you awake,
You will choose for your true love.
You will love and long for him,
Whether it be a lynx, a wildcat, or a bear, 30
A leopard, or a hog with bristled hair.
Whatever meets your eye
When you awake, it will be beloved.
Awake when some repulsive thing is near.

He exits.

LYSANDER *and* HERMIA *enter.*

LYSANDER

My beautiful love, you are weak from wandering in the woods. 35
And to tell the truth, I have forgotten which way to go.
Let us rest, Hermia, if you agree,
and wait for the comfort of daylight.

HERMIA

Let us do that, Lysander. Find a bed.
Upon this bank, I will rest my head. 40

LYSANDER

One piece of ground will serve as a bed for us both;
one heart, one bed, two bosoms, and one vow of love.

HERMIA

No, good Lysander. For my sake, my dear,
lie farther off. Do not lie so close.

LYSANDER

Please understand what I said in innocence, my sweet. 45
Lovers understand each other's real meaning when they speak.
I mean that my heart is joined with yours
so that together we have just one heart.

Two bosoms interchained with an oath—
50 So then two bosoms and a single troth.
Then by your side no bed-room me deny,
For lying so, Hermia, I do not lie.

HERMIA

Lysander riddles very prettily.
Now much beshrew* my manners and my pride
55 If Hermia meant to say Lysander lied.
But, gentle friend, for love and courtesy
Lie further off; in human modesty,
Such separation, as may well be said,
Becomes a virtuous bachelor and a maid,
60 So far be distant; and, good night, sweet friend.
Thy love ne'er alter till thy sweet life end!

LYSANDER

"Amen, amen," to that fair prayer, say I;
And then end life when I end loyalty!
Here is my bed. Sleep give thee all his rest!

HERMIA

65 With half that wish the wisher's eyes be press'd!

[*They sleep.*]

Enter ROBIN GOODFELLOW.

ROBIN GOODFELLOW

Through the forest have I gone,
But Athenian found I none,
On whose eyes I might approve
This flower's force in stirring love.
70 Night and silence!—Who is here?
Weeds of Athens he doth wear!
This is he, my master said,
Despised the Athenian maid.
And here the maiden, sleeping sound
75 On the dank and dirty ground.
Pretty soul, she durst not lie
Near this lack-love, this kill-courtesy.—

---

54 *beshrew* means "curse" but is usually meant lightly

Our two bosoms are chained together with a vow,
so we have two bosoms and one single love. 50
So don't refuse to allow me to sleep by your side.
For lying there beside you, Hermia, I would not be untrue.

HERMIA

Lysander, you make very nice riddles.
Now my manners and my pride should really be much cursed
if I meant to imply that you lied. 55
But, gentle friend, out of love and courtesy,
lie farther away, for the sake of human modesty.
It could well be said that such separation
is proper for a virtuous bachelor and a girl.
So keep your distance, and good night, sweet friend. 60
Never change your love as long as you live!

LYSANDER

Amen, amen, to that beautiful prayer I sing.
And may I die when I'm no longer loyal to you.
Here is my bed over here. May sleep give you all his rest.

HERMIA

I wish that half that wish may be pressed on the eyes of the
wisher! 65

They go to sleep.

PUCK *enters.*

PUCK

I have gone through the forest,
But I found no Athenian
On whose eyes I could test
This flower's power to cause love. (*He sees* LYSANDER.)
Night and silence! Who is this here? 70
He is wearing Athenian clothes.
This is the man who my master said
Despised the Athenian maiden.
And here is the maiden, sleeping soundly
On the damp and dirty ground. 75
She is a pretty soul. She does not dare lie
Near this man who doesn't love her, this rude man.

Churl, upon thy eyes I throw
All the power this charm doth owe.

[*He squeezes the flower on* LYSANDER's *eyelids.*]

80 When thou wak'st, let love forbid
Sleep his seat on thy eyelid;
So, awake when I am gone,
For I must now to Oberon.

[*Exit.*]

Enter DEMETRIUS *and* HELENA, *running.*

HELENA
Stay, though thou kill me, sweet Demetrius.

DEMETRIUS
85 I charge thee, hence, and do not haunt me thus.

HELENA
O, wilt thou darkling leave me? Do not so.

DEMETRIUS
Stay, on thy peril; I alone will go.

[DEMETRIUS *exits.*]

HELENA
O, I am out of breath in this fond chase!
The more my prayer, the lesser is my grace.
90 Happy is Hermia, wheresoe'er she lies,
For she hath blessed and attractive eyes.
How came her eyes so bright? Not with salt tears;
If so, my eyes are oft'ner wash'd than hers.
No, no, I am as ugly as a bear,
95 For beasts that meet me run away for fear.
Therefore no marvel though Demetrius
Do as a monster fly my presence thus.
What wicked and **dissembling** glass of mine
Made me compare with Hermia's sphery eyne?
100 But who is here? Lysander, on the ground!
Dead? or asleep? I see no blood, no wound.—
Lysander, if you live, good sir, awake.

Rascal, upon your eyes I throw
All the power this charm possesses.

(*He squeezes the flower on* LYSANDER's *eyelids.*)

When you awake, let love keep   80
Sleep from resting on your eyelids.
So awake when I have left,
For now I must go to Oberon.

He exits.

DEMETRIUS *and* HELENA *enter running.*

HELENA
Wait, even if you must kill me, sweet Demetrius.

DEMETRIUS
I order you, leave, and do not chase after me like this.   85

HELENA
Oh, will you leave me in the dark? Do not do so.

DEMETRIUS
Stay here, I'm warning you! I will go alone.

He exits.

HELENA
Oh, I am out of breath from this foolish chase.
The more I beg, the less I am forgiven.
Hermia is happy, wherever she lies,   90
because she has blessed and attractive eyes.
How did her eyes get to be so bright? Not from salty tears.
If that's the reason, my eyes are washed more often than hers.
No, no! I am as ugly as a bear,
because beasts that see me run away out of fear.   95
Therefore, it is no wonder that Demetrius
runs away from me as though I were a monster.
What wicked and lying mirror
made me compare my eyes with Hermia's starry eyes?
But who is this? Lysander! Here on the ground.   100
Is he dead? or asleep? I see no blood, no wound.
Lysander, if you are alive, good sir, wake up.

LYSANDER [*awaking*]

And run through fire I will for thy sweet sake.
Transparent Helena! Nature shows art,

105 That through thy bosom makes me see thy heart.
Where is Demetrius? O, how fit a word
Is that vile name to perish on my sword!

HELENA

Do not say so, Lysander; say not so.
What though he love your Hermia? Lord, what though?

110 Yet Hermia still loves you; then be content.

LYSANDER

Content with Hermia? No, I do repent
The tedious minutes I with her have spent.
Not Hermia but Helena I love.
Who will not change a raven for a dove?

115 The will of man is by his reason sway'd,
And reason says you are the worthier maid.
Things growing are not ripe until their season;
So I, being young, till now ripe not to reason.
And touching now the point of human skill,

120 Reason becomes the marshal to my will
And leads me to your eyes, where I o'erlook
Love's stories written in love's richest book.

HELENA

Wherefore was I to this keen mockery born?
When at your hands did I deserve this scorn?

125 Is 't not enough, is 't not enough, young man,
That I did never, no, nor never can,
Deserve a sweet look from Demetrius's eye,
But you must flout my insufficiency?
Good troth, you do me wrong, good sooth you do,

130 In such disdainful manner me to woo.
But fare you well; perforce I must confess
I thought you lord of more true gentleness.

LYSANDER (*awakening*)

And I will run through fire for your sweet sake.
Brilliantly beautiful Helena, nature teaches understanding,
so that through your bosom, I can see your heart.   105
Where is Demetrius? Oh, how fitting it
would be for that disgusting name to die by my sword.

HELENA

Don't say that, Lysander; don't say that.
What does it matter that he loves your Hermia? Lord, what does it
     matter?
Hermia still loves you, so be happy.   110

LYSANDER

Happy with Hermia? No. I repent
the tedious minutes I have spent with her.
It is not Hermia, but you, Helena, whom I love.
Who wouldn't trade a raven for a dove?
Man's desires are often swayed by his reason,   115
and my reason says you are the better woman.
Fruit does not ripen until it is ready.
So I, being young, have not had mature understandings until now.
But now that I have reached a maturity of human reason,
reason becomes the guide of my will,   120
and leads me to your eyes. There I see
love's stories, written in love's richest book.

HELENA

Why was I born to bear this biting mockery?
What did I do to deserve this scorn from you?
Isn't it enough, isn't it enough, young man,   125
that I never did—no, nor ever could—
deserve a sweet look from Demetrius's eyes,
but that you, too, make fun of my inadequacies?
Really, you do me wrong! Indeed you do
to speak of love to me in such a contemptible manner.   130
Goodbye. I must confess that
I thought you were a more honestly noble man.

O, that a lady, of one man refus'd,
Should of another therefore be abus'd!

[*She exits.*]

LYSANDER
135 She sees not Hermia.—Hermia, sleep thou there,
And never mayst thou come Lysander near!
For as a **surfeit** of the sweetest things
The deepest loathing to the stomach brings,
Or as the heresies that men do leave
140 Are hated most of those they did deceive,
So thou, my surfeit and my heresy,
Of all be hated, but the most of me!
And, all my powers, address your love and might
To honour Helen and to be her knight.

[*He exits.*]

HERMIA [*awaking*]
145 Help me, Lysander, help me! Do thy best
To pluck this crawling serpent from my breast.
Ay me, for pity! What a dream was here!
Lysander, look how I do quake with fear.
Methought a serpent ate my heart away,
150 And you sat smiling at his cruel prey.
Lysander! What, remov'd? Lysander, lord!
What, out of hearing? Gone? No sound, no word?
Alack, where are you? Speak, an if you hear.
Speak, of all loves! I swoon almost with fear.—
155 No? Then I well perceive you are not nigh.
Either death or you I'll find immediately.

[*Exit.*]

It is too bad that a lady, refused by one man,
should therefore be abused by another.

> *She exits.*

LYSANDER
She didn't see Hermia. Hermia, stay asleep over there,   135
and don't ever come near me.
Just as gorging on sweet things
makes you sick of the taste,
or as the heresies that men speak
are hated most by those they deceived,   140
so, you Hermia, are my gorging and my heresy,
hated by all, but most of all by me!
Now, Lysander, use all your powers and your love and strength
to honor Helen and be her knight!

> *He exits.*

HERMIA (*awakening*)
Help me, Lysander, help me! Please   145
pull this crawling snake from my breast!
Oh me, for pity's sake, what a dream I had!
Lysander, see how I'm shaking with fear.
I thought a snake ate my heart away,
and you sat smiling at his cruel act.   150
Lysander! What, are you gone? Lysander! Lord!
What, are you out of hearing? Gone? Not a sound, not a word?
Alas, where are you? Speak, if you can hear me.
Speak for love's sake. I am almost fainting with fear.
No? Then I can see you are not nearby.   155
I'll find either you or death immediately.

> *She exits.*

Act II Review

Discussion Questions

1. Some people believe that by having Lysander first love Hermia, and then suddenly switch his devotion to Helena, Shakespeare is saying that love is an accident and that a person might as easily love one person as another. Do you think this is Shakespeare's message? Explain.

2. Helena says of her sex, "We cannot fight for love, as men may do. / We should be woo'd and were not made to woo." Discuss what this means. How much do you think this attitude has changed since Shakespeare's time?

3. In Scene ii, the fairies make a brief appearance to sing Titania to sleep. Discuss what purpose this scene might serve in the play.

4. Consider Oberon's behavior in this act, especially his instructions to Puck to use the magic potion on both Titania and Demetrius. What does this say about his motivations and character?

5. What similarities and differences do you see between the attitudes and actions of Egeus (Hermia's father) in Act I and Oberon in Act II?

Literary Elements

1. Look for an example of **exposition**—information that is expressed directly rather than shown or implied—in Act II. How else could that information be conveyed?

2. Identify some of the magical elements in Scene i and tell how they contribute to the **mood**, or atmosphere, of the play.

3. **Irony** refers to the difference between what is expected and what actually happens. How is love viewed ironically in Acts I and II?

Writing Prompts

1. Rewrite the scene between Demetrius and Helena (Scene i, lines 192–248) in contemporary, informal language with a modern setting, such as a shopping mall or high school hallway.

2. Using what you know from both acts so far, compare and contrast the personalities of the four young lovers: Hermia, Helena, Lysander, and Demetrius. Use a chart to list their characteristics; then write a summary of your conclusions.

3. Pretend you are an advice columnist for the *Athenian Times* during the period of the play. Helena has written asking what she should do about her unrequited love for Demetrius. Write your advice to her in Shakespeare's language.

4. Choose a quotation from Scene i or ii that you feel best characterizes that scene. In a paragraph, discuss why you think the quotation is significant and effective at conveying the events or themes of that scene.

A Midsummer Night's Dream

ACT III

Kevin Kline as Nick Bottom and Michelle Pfeiffer as Titania, 1999 film of the play

*"What angel wakes me
from my flowery bed?"*

Before You Read

1. Considering the events in the fairy kingdom, the action among the workmen/actors and the young lovers, and the upcoming wedding festivities, much has been going on. What do you think are two of the most significant events so far? Explain why.

2. Puck has been careless with his magic potions. Do you think he made an honest mistake when he put the drops in Lysander's eyes, or did he cause more confusion among the mortals on purpose? Explain.

3. What do you think it might take to persuade Helena that Lysander is not making fun of her but is truly in love with her?

Literary Elements

1. The struggle between opposing forces, or desires, creates **conflict.** This play is full of romantic conflict; Hermia's father wants her to marry Demetrius, Hermia wants to marry Lysander, Demetrius wants to marry Hermia, Lysander wants to marry Helena, and Helena wants to marry Demetrius.

2. A **comedy** entertains its audience with a lighthearted or satirical tone, and by convention the plot often ends with a marriage ceremony. In Shakespeare's comedies, romantic love is often thwarted by the wishes of a young person's father, in this play, Hermia's father, Egeus.

3. Comedy, tragedy, allegory, and epic are among the many types, or **genres**, of literature. *A Midsummer Night's Dream* is clearly a comedy, but it also has elements of other genres, for example, fairy tale, romance, and satire.

Words to Know

The following vocabulary words appear in Act III in the original text of
Shakespeare's play. However, they are words that are still used today.
Read the definitions here and pay attention to the words as you read the
play (they will be in boldfaced type).

abate	cut short; reduce
congealed	frozen; solidified
conjure	bring up; invoke
consecrated	made sacred; devoted to a special purpose
derision	mockery; ridicule
disparage	put down; degrade
gambol	skip; leap
odious	foul; revolting
rebuke	scold; criticize
recompense	payment; compensation

Act Summary

As Queen Titania awakens, the group of actors is rehearsing. The first
creature she sees is Nick Bottom, a weaver, whose head has been
transformed by Puck into a donkey's head. Because of the potion, she
falls in love with a dazed but pleased Bottom, dotes on him, and orders
the Fairies to wait upon him.

Because Lysander has disappeared from her side, Hermia accuses
Demetrius of having killed his rival. When Oberon hears their
conversation, he realizes Puck has made a mistake. He tells Puck to bring
Helena to Demetrius through magic.

While Puck goes on his errand, Oberon drops the potion into
Demetrius's eyes so that he will fall in love with Helena when she arrives.
The plan succeeds, so both men are now madly in love with Helena,
much to the delight of the whimsical Puck. Helena is convinced that

Demetrius, Lysander, and Hermia have all collaborated to mock and humiliate her. The rivals insist that they are sincere and in fact are spoiling for a fight to determine who wins Helena.

A shocked Hermia is brokenhearted because Lysander no longer loves her. So King Oberon instructs Puck to lead Lysander and Demetrius away from each other to prevent them from fighting. He gives Puck an herb to crush into Lysander's eyes as he sleeps, to take away the magic spell that has made him love Helena. If all goes well, Lysander and Hermia should soon be reunited.

Paul Rudd, Toni Wein, Richard Gere, and Lucy Lee Flippin, Lincoln Center for the Performing Arts, New York, 1970s

ACT III, SCENE I

[The wood, TITANIA *lying asleep.] Enter the* CLOWNS
[QUINCE, SNUG, BOTTOM, FLUTE, SNOUT, *and*
STARVELING].

BOTTOM
Are we all met?

QUINCE
Pat, pat. And here's a marvels convenient place for our
rehearsal. This green plot shall be our stage, this hawthorn
brake our tiring-house, and we will do it in action as we
5   will do it before the Duke.

BOTTOM
Peter Quince!

QUINCE
What say'st thou, bully Bottom?

BOTTOM
There are things in this comedy of Pyramus and Thisbe
that will never please. First, Pyramus must draw a sword
10   to kill himself, which the ladies cannot abide. How
answer you that?

SNOUT
By 'r lakin,* a parlous fear.

STARVELING
I believe we must leave the killing out, when all is done.

BOTTOM
Not a whit! I have a device to make all well. Write me a
15   prologue, and let the prologue seem to say we will do no
harm with our swords, and that Pyramus is not kill'd
indeed. And, for the more better assurance, tell them that
I, Pyramus, am not Pyramus, but Bottom the weaver. This
will put them out of fear.

---

12   *lakin* a corruption of lady kin, or little lady, and reference to the Virgin Mary

ACT 3, SCENE 1

The woods. TITANIA *is lying asleep.* QUINCE, SNUG, BOTTOM, FLUTE, SNOUT, *and* STARVELING *all enter.*

BOTTOM

Are we all here?

QUINCE

Exactly, exactly. And here's a marvelously convenient place for us to rehearse. This grassy spot will be our stage, this hawthorn thicket our dressing room, and we'll perform it exactly like we'll do it before the Duke.   5

BOTTOM

Peter Quince!

QUINCE

What do you want, good fellow, Bottom?

BOTTOM

There are things in this comedy of Pyramus and Thisbe that will never be appealing. First, Pyramus must draw a sword to kill himself, which the ladies would never like. What do you say   10
about that?

SNOUT

By Our Lady, that is a terrible problem!

STARVELING

I think we'd better leave the killing out, after all.

BOTTOM

Not at all. I have a way to make everything turn out fine. Write me a prologue, and let the prologue imply that we will do no harm   15
with our swords, and that Pyramus is not really killed. To give them even more reassurance, tell them that I, the one playing Pyramus, am not Pyramus but Bottom the weaver. That will keep them from being afraid.

QUINCE

20   Well, we will have such a prologue, and it shall be written
in eight and six.*

BOTTOM

No, make it two more. Let it be written in eight and eight.

SNOUT

Will not the ladies be afeard of the lion?

STARVELING

I fear it, I promise you.

BOTTOM

25   Masters, you ought to consider with yourself, to bring in—
God shield us!—a lion among ladies, is a most dreadful
thing. For there is not a more fearful wild fowl than your
lion living; and we ought to look to 't.

SNOUT

Therefore another prologue must tell he is not a lion.

BOTTOM

30   Nay, you must name his name, and half his face must be
seen through the lion's neck, and he himself must speak
through, saying thus, or to the same defect*: "Ladies," or
"Fair ladies, I would wish you," or "I would request you,"
or "I would entreat you not to fear, not to tremble! My life

35   for yours. If you think I come hither as a lion, it were pity
of my life. No, I am no such thing; I am a man as other
men are." And there indeed let him name his name and
tell them plainly he is Snug the joiner.

QUINCE

Well, it shall be so. But there is two hard things: that is, to

40   bring the moonlight into a chamber, for, you know,
Pyramus and Thisbe meet by moonlight.

SNOUT

Doth the moon shine that night we play our play?

---

21   *eight and six* ballads consist of alternating lines of eight and six syllables

32   *defect* Bottom's malapropism for "effect"

QUINCE

All right, we will have such a prologue, and it shall be in lines of   20
eight and six syllables.

BOTTOM

No, make it two more syllables. Let it be written in eight and eight
syllables.

SNOUT

Won't the ladies be afraid of the lion?

STARVELING

I'm afraid they will, I swear.

BOTTOM

Masters, you should think this over. To bring in—God help   25
us!—a lion among ladies is a most dreadful thing.
For there is not a more fearful wild fowl alive than a lion.
And we should do something about it.

SNOUT

Therefore, another prologue must say that he's not a lion.

BOTTOM

No, you must give his name, and half his face must be seen   30
through the lion's neck, and he himself must speak,
saying this—or something to the same defect: "Ladies," or
"Lovely ladies, I wish you," or "I request you," or "I beg you not to
be afraid or tremble. I'd give my life for yours. If you think I   35
come here as a lion, it would be my head on the block. No! I'm no
such thing. I'm a man just like other men." And at that point, let
him give his name and tell them plainly that he is Snug the joiner.

QUINCE

Well, we'll do it like that. But there still are two problems. One is
how to make the moonlight fall into the hall because, you   40
know, Pyramus and Thisbe meet by moonlight.

SNOUT

Does the moon shine the night we play our play?

BOTTOM

A calendar, a calendar! Look in the almanac! Find out
moonshine, find out moonshine.

QUINCE

45 Yes, it doth shine that night.

BOTTOM

Why, then may you leave a casement of the great chamber
window, where we play, open, and the moon may shine in
at the casement.

QUINCE

Ay, or else one must come in with a bush of thorns and a
50 lantern and say he comes to disfigure or to present the
person of Moonshine.* Then there is another thing: we
must have a wall in the great chamber, for Pyramus and
Thisbe, says the story, did talk through the chink of a wall.

SNOUT

You can never bring in a wall. What say you, Bottom?

BOTTOM

55 Some man or other must present Wall; and let him have
some plaster, or some loam, or some rough-cast about
him to signify wall, or let him hold his fingers thus, and
through that cranny shall Pyramus and Thisbe whisper.

QUINCE

If that may be, then all is well. Come, sit down, every
60 mother's son, and rehearse your parts. Pyramus, you
begin. When you have spoken your speech, enter into that
brake, and so every one according to his cue.

Enter ROBIN GOODFELLOW *behind.*

ROBIN GOODFELLOW [*aside*]

What hempen homespuns have we swagg'ring here,
So near the cradle of the Fairy Queen?
65 What, a play toward! I'll be an auditor—
An actor too perhaps, if I see cause.

49–51 *bush . . . Moonshine* According to some tales, the man in the moon was
sentenced to live on the moon because he collected firewood on Sunday, a
holy day.

BOTTOM

A calendar, get a calendar! Look in the almanac. Find out if the moon shines; find out if the moon shines! (QUINCE *searches through the almanac.*)

QUINCE

Yes, it shines that night.   45

BOTTOM

Well, then you may leave a window open in the large hall where we'll put on our play, and the moon will shine in through the window.

QUINCE

Yes, or else one of us must come in with a bush of thorns and a lantern and say that he comes to disfigure or represent the   50 character Moonshine. Then there is another thing. We must have a wall in the great hall because Pyramus and Thisbe talked through a crack in the wall, according to the story.

SNOUT

You can never bring in a wall. What do you say, Bottom?

BOTTOM

Someone or other must pretend to be the wall. And he should   55 have some plaster, or some soil, or some plaster and pebbles covering him to show that he is a wall. And let him hold his fingers like this. Through that crack, Pyramus and Thisbe will whisper.

QUINCE

If we do that, all will be well. Come, sit down, every mother's son of you. Rehearse your parts. Pyramus, you begin. When you   60 have delivered your speech, go into that thicket. Everyone else do the scene according to your cue.

> PUCK *enters.*

PUCK (*aside*)

What kind of crude yokels do we have swaggering here, so near the bed of the Fairy Queen? What's this? A play about to begin? I'll be a listener—   65 an actor, too, perhaps—if I see a chance.

QUINCE

Speak, Pyramus.—Thisbe, stand forth.

BOTTOM [*as* PYRAMUS]

"Thisbe, the flowers of **odious** savours sweet"—

QUINCE

Odours, odours!

BOTTOM [*as* PYRAMUS]

70   —"Odours savours sweet.

So hath thy breath, my dearest Thisbe dear.—

But hark, a voice! Stay thou but here awhile,

And by and by I will to thee appear."

[*Exit.*]

ROBIN GOODFELLOW

A stranger Pyramus than e'er played here.

[*Exit.*]

FLUTE

75   Must I speak now?

QUINCE

Ay, marry, must you, for you must understand he goes but
to see a noise that he heard and is to come again.

FLUTE [*as* THISBE]

"Most radiant Pyramus, most lily-white of hue,

Of colour like the red rose on triumphant brier,

80   Most brisky juvenal and eke most lovely Jew,*

As true as truest horse that yet would never tire,

I'll meet thee, Pyramus, at Ninny's tomb."

QUINCE

"Ninus's* tomb," man! Why, you must not speak that yet.
That you answer to Pyramus. You speak all your part at

85   once, cues and all.—Pyramus enter. Your cue is past; it is,
"never tire."

FLUTE [*as* THISBE]

O!—"As true as truest horse, that yet would never tire."

---

80   *Jew* probably Thisbe's meaningless attempt to repeat the sound of "juvenal"

83   *Ninus* the ruler of Babylon (and locale of the troop's play)

QUINCE
Speak, Pyramus. Thisbe, come forward.

BOTTOM, *as* PYRAMUS
Thisbe, the flowers have odious sweet aromas—

QUINCE
Odorous! Odorous!

BOTTOM, *as* PYRAMUS
Odor's sweet aromas. 70
So does your breath, my dearest Thisbe dear.
But listen, a voice! You stay here awhile.
And soon I will be back.

> *He exits.*

PUCK (*aside*)
Never before has a stranger Pyramus than this been played!

> *He exits.*

FLUTE
Should I speak now? 75

QUINCE
Yes, indeed you should. For you see he's just going to
investigate a noise that he heard. He will be back.

FLUTE, *as* THISBE
Most radiant Pyramus, so lily-white,
You are the color of a red rose on a triumphant brier.
You are a most lively youth, and also a most lovely Jew. 80
You are as true as the truest horse that never tires,
I'll meet you, Pyramus, at Ninny's tomb.

QUINCE
"Ninus's tomb," man! Why, you mustn't say that yet. That is your
response to Pyramus. You speak all of your part at once, cues 85
and all. Pyramus, enter. Your cue has past. It is "never tire."

FLUTE, *as* THISBE
Oh—as true as truest horse that never tires.

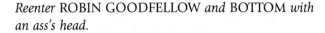

Reenter ROBIN GOODFELLOW *and* BOTTOM *with an ass's head.*

BOTTOM [*as* PYRAMUS]
"If I were fair, fair Thisbe, I were only thine."

QUINCE
O monstrous! O strange! We are haunted.
90 Pray, masters, fly, masters! Help!

Exeunt QUINCE, SNUG, FLUTE, SNOUT, *and* STARVELING.

ROBIN GOODFELLOW
I'll follow you, I'll lead you about a round,
  Through bog, through bush, through brake, through
    brier.
Sometime a horse I'll be, sometime a hound,
  A hog, a headless bear, sometime a fire;
95 And neigh, and bark, and grunt, and roar, and burn,
Like horse, hound, hog, bear, fire, at every turn.

[*Exit.*]

BOTTOM
Why do they run away? This is a knavery of them to make
me afeard.

Reenter Snout.

SNOUT
O Bottom, thou art chang'd! What do I see on thee?

BOTTOM
100 What do you see? You see an ass-head of your own, do you?

[*Exit Snout.*]

Reenter Quince.

QUINCE
Bless thee, Bottom, bless thee! Thou art translated!

[*Exit.*]

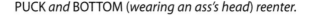

PUCK *and* BOTTOM (*wearing an ass's head*) *reenter.*

BOTTOM, *as* PYRAMUS
If I were handsome, Thisbe, I would be yours alone.

QUINCE *sees* BOTTOM *with the ass's head.*

QUINCE
Oh this is monstrous! Strange! We are haunted.
Please, gentlemen! Run, gentlemen! Help!   90

They all exit, except BOTTOM.

PUCK
I'll follow you. I'll lead you roundabaout
   Through swamp, through bushes, through thickets, through
      briers.
Sometimes I'll be a horse, sometimes a hound,
  a hog, a headless bear, sometimes a fire.
I'll neigh, and bark, and grunt, and roar, and burn,   95
like a horse, hound, hog, bear, and fire at every turn.

He exits.

BOTTOM
Why are they running away? This is mean of them to scare me.

SNOUT *enters.*

SNOUT
Oh, Bottom, you have changed! What do I see on you?

BOTTOM
What do you see? You're making an ass out of yourself trying   100
to make one of me, aren't you?

SNOUT *exits.*

QUINCE *enters.*

QUINCE
Heavens, Bottom! Heavens! You've been transformed.

QUINCE *exits.*

BOTTOM

I see their knavery; this is to make an ass of me, to fright me, if they could. But I will not stir from this place, do what they can. I will walk up and down here, and I will sing, that they shall hear I am not afraid.

[*Sings.*]

"The ouzel cock, so black of hue,
    With orange-tawny bill,
The throstle with his note so true,
    The wren with little quill"—*

TITANIA [*awaking*]

What angel wakes me from my flowery bed?

BOTTOM [*Sings.*]

"The finch, the sparrow, and the lark,
    The plain-song cuckoo* gray,
Whose note full many a man doth mark,
    And dares not answer nay"—

for, indeed, who would set his wit to so fooling a bird? Who would give a bird the lie though he cry "cuckoo" never so?

TITANIA

I pray thee, gentle mortal, sing again.
Mine ear is much enamour'd of thy note;
So is mine eye enthralled to thy shape;
And thy fair virtue's force perforce doth move me
On the first view to say, to swear, I love thee.

BOTTOM

Methinks, mistress, you should have little reason for that. And yet, to say the truth, reason and love keep little company together nowadays. The more the pity that some honest neighbours will not make them friends. Nay, I can gleek upon occasion.

TITANIA

Thou art as wise as thou art beautiful.

---

109 *quill* a musical reed pipe

112 *cuckoo* The song of the cuckoo supposedly told a man if he was a cuckold, a man whose wife is an adulteress. "Cuckoo" and "cuckold" sound alike.

BOTTOM

I see what mischief they're up to. They're doing this to make an ass of me, to frighten me, as if they could. But I won't budge from this place, no matter what they do. I will walk up and down here, and I will sing so that they shall hear that I am not afraid: 105

(*He sings.*)

The blackbird is very black
*   And has an orange-tawny bill.*
The thrush has a note so true.
*   The wren has a high voice—*

TITANIA (*awakening*)

What angel awakes me from my flowery bed? 110

BOTTOM (*singing*)

The finch, the sparrow, and the lark,
*   The simple-singing gray cuckoo,*
To whose note many a man listens
*   And dares not deny—*

For, indeed, who would try to reason out an answer to such a 115
foolish bird? Who would contradict a bird, even if he does cry
"cuckoo" as never before?

TITANIA

I beg you, gentle mortal, sing again.
My ear is very much attracted to your song.
My eye also is enslaved by your looks.
And the power of your wonderful character moves me
to say, to swear, that after just one look—I love you. 120

BOTTOM

I think, my lady, that you have little reason for that. And yet,
to tell you the truth, reason and love aren't often found
together these days. It's a pity that some honest neighbors 125
will not make them friends. You see, I can make a satirical joke
upon occasion.

TITANIA

You are as wise as you are beautiful.

BOTTOM

Not so, neither; but if I had wit enough to get out of this
130 wood, I have enough to serve mine own turn.

TITANIA

Out of this wood do not desire to go;
Thou shalt remain here, whether thou wilt or no.
I am a spirit of no common rate.
The summer still doth tend upon my state,
135 And I do love thee; therefore, go with me.
I'll give thee fairies to attend on thee,
And thy shall fetch thee jewels from the deep,
And sing while thou on pressed flowers dost sleep.
And I will purge thy mortal grossness so
140 That thou shalt like an airy spirit go.—
Peaseblossom! Cobweb! Moth!* And Mustardseed!

> *Enter four* FAIRIES, PEASEBLOSSOM, COBWEB,
> MOTH, *and* MUSTARDSEED.

PEASEBLOSSOM

Ready.

COBWEB

And I.

MOTH

And I.

MUSTARDSEED

145 And I.

ALL

Where shall we go?

TITANIA

Be kind and courteous to this gentleman.
Hop in his walks and **gambol** in his eyes;
Feed him with apricocks and dewberries,
150 With purple grapes, green figs, and mulberries;
The honey-bags steal from the humble-bees,
And for night-tapers crop their waxen thighs

---

141 *Moth* sometimes named "mote" (a small speck of dust) rather than the insect
the moth

BOTTOM

That isn't true either. But if I had enough intelligence to get
out of this woods, I'd have enough to suit myself.   130

TITANIA

Don't desire to leave this woods.
You shall remain here whether you want to or not.
I am no spirit of common rank—
the summer always waits upon me.
And I do love you. Therefore, come with me.   135
I'll give you fairies to wait upon you.
They shall bring you jewels from the deep sea
and sing while you sleep on pressed flowers.
And I will so purify your human grossness,
that you will be able to move like an airy spirit.   140
Peaseblossom! Cobweb! Moth! Mustardseed!

Four FAIRIES *enter:* PEASEBLOSSOM, COBWEB, MOTH, *and*
MUSTARDSEED.

PEASEBLOSSOM

At your service.

COBWEB

And I.

MOTH

And I.

MUSTARDSEED

And I.   145

ALL

Where do you want us to go?

TITANIA

Be kind and courteous to this gentleman.
Hop in his walks and frolic in his eyes.
Feed him with apricots, blackberries,
purple grapes, green figs, and mulberries.   150
Steal the honey bags from the bumblebees,
and for night candles, cut off their waxen thighs

And light them at the fiery glowworm's eyes,
To have my love to bed and to arise;
155 And pluck the wings from painted butterflies
To fan the moonbeams from his sleeping eyes.
Nod to him, elves, and do him courtesies.

PEASEBLOSSOM
Hail, mortal!

COBWEB
Hail!

MOTH
160 Hail!

MUSTARDSEED
Hail!

BOTTOM
I cry your Worship's mercy, heartily.—I beseech your
Worship's name.

COBWEB
Cobweb.

BOTTOM
165 I shall desire you of more acquaintance, good Master
Cobweb. If I cut my finger, I shall make bold with you.*—
Your name, honest gentleman?

PEASEBLOSSOM
Peaseblossom.

BOTTOM
I pray you commend me to Mistress Squash,* your
170 mother, and to Master Peascod,* your father. Good Master
Peaseblossom, I shall desire you of more acquaintance
too.—Your name, I beseech you, sir?

MUSTARDSEED
Mustardseed.

---

166 *I shall make bold with you.* Cobwebs were used to stop bleeding.

169 *Squash* an unripe peapod

170 *Peascod* a ripe peapod

and light them from the fiery glowworm's eyes
to light my love the way to bed and to arise.
Pluck the wings from painted butterflies   155
to fan the moonbeams from his sleeping eyes.
Bow to him, elves, and serve him courteously.

PEASEBLOSSOM
Greetings, mortal!

COBWEB
Greetings!

MOTH
Greetings!   160

MUSTARDSEED
Greetings!

BOTTOM
I heartily beg your pardon, your Honor. Please tell me your
name, your Worship.

COBWEB
Cobweb.

BOTTOM
I want to get to know you better, good Master Cobweb.   165
If I cut my finger, I will have to ask for your help. What is your
name, honest gentleman?

PEASEBLOSSOM
Peaseblossom.

BOTTOM
I beg you, give my regards to Mistress Squash, your mother, and
to Master Peascod, your father. Good Master Peaseblossom,   170
I want to get to know you better, too. What is your name
please, sir?

MUSTARDSEED
Mustardseed.

BOTTOM

Good Master Mustardseed, I know your patience well.
175 That same cowardly, giantlike ox-beef hath devoured
many a gentleman of your house.* I promise you, your
kindred hath made my eyes water ere now. I desire you
more acquaintance, good Master Mustardseed.

TITANIA

Come, wait upon him; lead him to my bower.
180 The moon methinks looks with a wat'ry eye;
And when she weeps, weeps every little flower,
Lamenting some enforced chastity.
Tie up my love's tongue; bring him silently.

[*Exeunt.*]

175-76 *ox-beef . . . house* Mustard was frequently eaten with beef.

BOTTOM

Good Master Mustardseed, I'm well aware of your patient
suffering. The cowardly, giantlike ox-beef has devoured many   175
gentlemen from your house. I swear to you, your relatives have
made my eyes water before now. I want to get to know you
better, good Master Mustardseed.

TITANIA

Come, take care of him. Lead him to my bedroom.
    I think the moon is gazing on the world with a watery eye.   180
And when she cries, every little flower cries,
    Mourning that someone's virginity has been violated.
Tie up my lover's tongue and bring him silently.

    All exit.

ACT III, SCENE II

[*Another part of the wood.*] *Enter* OBERON.

OBERON
> I wonder if Titania be awak'd;
> Then, what it was that next came in her eye,
> Which she must dote on in extremity.

> *Enter* ROBIN GOODFELLOW.

> Here comes my messenger. How now, mad spirit!
5 > What night-rule now about this haunted grove?

ROBIN GOODFELLOW
> My mistress with a monster is in love.
> Near to her close and **consecrated** bower,
> While she was in her dull and sleeping hour,
> A crew of patches, rude mechanicals,
10 > That work for bread upon Athenian stalls,
> Were met together to rehearse a play
> Intended for great Theseus's nuptial day.
> The shallowest thickskin of that barren sort,
> Who Pyramus presented in their sport,
15 > Forsook his scene and ent'red in a brake.
> When I did him at this advantage take,
> An ass's noll I fixed on his head.
> Anon his Thisbe must be answered,
> And forth my mimic comes. When they him spy,
20 > As wild geese that the creeping fowler eye,
> Or russet-pated choughs, many in sort,
> Rising and cawing at the gun's report,
> Sever themselves and madly sweep the sky,
> So at his sight away his fellows fly;
25 > And, at our stamp, here o'er and o'er one falls;
> He "Murder!" cries and help from Athens calls.
> Their sense thus weak, lost with their fears thus strong,
> Made senseless things begin to do them wrong;
> For briers and thorns at their apparel snatch,
30 > Some sleeves, some hats, from yielders all things catch.
> I led them on in this distracted fear

ACT 3, SCENE 2

Another part of the forest. OBERON *enters.*

OBERON

I wonder if Titania has awakened.
If so, I would so like to know what she first saw,
which she must love to the extreme?

    PUCK *enters.*

Here comes my messenger. What's going on, mad spirit?
What is happening tonight in this haunted woods?   5

PUCK

My mistress is in love with a monster.
Near her private and consecrated bower,
while she was resting and sleeping,
there came a group of fools—uneducated artisans,
who work for bread in Athens.   10
They had come together to rehearse a play
to be presented on the great Theseus's wedding day.
The shallowest country clown in that stupid crew—
who played Pyramus in their little play—
left the "stage" and entered into the thicket.   15
When I was able to catch him at this opportunity,
I secured an ass's head on his shoulders.
Soon he had to answer his Thisbe in the play
and so out comes my clown. When they saw him,
they ran like wild geese who see the eye of a concealed hunter.   20
Or like a large flock of brown-headed jackdaws—
taking off and cawing when the gun goes off,
separating themselves and madly sweeping the sky—
just in that manner his friends flew away at the sight of him.
And because of my creature, one of them tumbled over.   25
Another cried, "Murder," and called for help from Athens.
With their weak brains, and consumed by intense fear,
they imagined that objects could harm them
because briers and thorns snatched at their clothes.
Some were caught by their sleeves and hats—cowards are   30
    attacked by everything.
I led them on this state of wild fear

And left sweet Pyramus translated there;
When in that moment, so it came to pass,
Titania wak'd and straightway lov'd an ass.

OBERON

35 This falls out better than I could devise.
But hast thou yet latch'd the Athenian's eyes
With the love juice, and I did bid thee do?

ROBIN GOODFELLOW

I took him sleeping—that is finish'd, too—
And the Athenian woman by his side;
40 That, when he wak'd, of force she must be ey'd.

Enter DEMETRIUS *and* HERMIA.

OBERON

Stand close. This is the same Athenian.

ROBIN GOODFELLOW

This is the woman, but not this the man.

DEMETRIUS

O, why **rebuke** you him that loves you so?
Lay breath so bitter on your bitter foe!

HERMIA

45 Now I but chide; but I should use thee worse,
For thou, I fear, hast given me cause to curse.
If thou hast slain Lysander in his sleep,
Being o'er shoes in blood, plunge in the deep
And kill me too.
50 The sun was not so true unto the day
As he to me. Would he have stolen away
From sleeping Hermia? I'll believe as soon
This whole earth may be bor'd and that the moon
May through the centre creep and so displease
55 Her brother's* noontide with th' Antipodes.*
It cannot be but thou hast murd'red him;
So should a murderer look, so dread so grim.

---

55 *brother* The sun god was the brother of the moon goddess in Greek mythology.

55 *Antipodes* region on the other side of the world

and left sweet Pyramus changed there.
In that moment, it so happened
that Titania awakened and right away fell in love with an ass.

OBERON

This worked out better than I could have planned it. 35
But have you smeared the Athenian's eyes
with the love juice, as I ordered you to do?

PUCK

I caught him sleeping, so that is finished, too.
And the Athenian woman was by his side
so that when he wakes up, by necessity, she will be seen. 40

DEMETRIUS *and* HERMIA *enter.*

OBERON

Hide. This is that very Athenian.

PUCK

This is the woman I was talking about, but this is not the man.

DEMETRIUS

Oh why do you scold the man who loves you so much?
Save your bitter words for your bitter enemy.

HERMIA

I am only scolding now, but I should treat you worse, 45
for you, I'm afraid, have given me reason to curse.
If you killed Lysander in his sleep,
and walked ankle-deep in his blood, go ahead
and kill me too.
The sun was not as true to the day 50
as he is to me. Would he have sneaked away
from his sleeping Hermia? I'd as soon believe
that the solid world could be drilled straight through and that the
    moon
could creep through the center and disrupt
her brother's noontime for the Antipodes. 55
It has to be that you have murdered him.
You look like a murderer—so deathly pale, so grim.

DEMETRIUS

So should the murder'd look, and so should I,
Pierc'd through the heart with your stern cruelty;
60 Yet you, the murderer, look as bright, as clear,
As yonder Venus in her glimmering sphere.

HERMIA

What's this to my Lysander? Where is he?
Ah, good Demetrius, wilt thou give him me?

DEMETRIUS

I had rather give his carcass to my hounds.

HERMIA

65 Out, dog! Out, cur! Thou driv'st me past the bounds
Of maiden's patience. Hast thou slain him, then?
Henceforth be never numb'red among men!
O, once tell true! Tell true, even for my sake!
Durst thou have look'd upon him, being awake?
70 And has thou kill'd him sleeping? O brave touch!
Could not a worm, an adder, do so much?
An adder did it; for with doubler tongue
Than thine, thou serpent, never adder stung.

DEMETRIUS

You spend your passion on a mispris'd mood.
75 I am not guilty of Lysander's blood;
Nor is he dead, for aught that I can tell.

HERMIA

I pray thee, tell me then that he is well.

DEMETRIUS

An if I could, what should I get therefore?

HERMIA

A privilege never to see me more.
80 And from thy hated presence part I so:
See me no more, whether he be dead or no.

    [Exit.]

DEMETRIUS

There is no following her in this fierce vein;

DEMETRIUS

That is the way the murdered should look, and so should I.
I am pierced through the heart by your stern cruelty.
Yet you, the murderer, look as bright and clear   60
as Venus over there in her glimmering orbit.

HERMIA

What does this have to do with my Lysander? Where is he?
Good Demetrius, won't you give him to me?

DEMETRIUS

I'd rather give his dead body to my hounds.

HERMIA

Get away, you dog! Away, you cur! You're driving me beyond   65
        the bounds
of my maidenly patience. Have you killed him, then?
From now on, you should never be called a man.
Tell me the truth just for once! Tell me the truth, for my sake.
Would you have even dared look at him if he was awake?
And did you kill him while he slept? What a noble exploit!   70
Couldn't a snake or an adder do the same?
An adder did do it, for with never a more double tongue
than yours, you snake, did an adder ever sting.

DEMETRIUS

You're wasting your energy in mistaken anger.
I am not guilty of killing Lysander.   75
Nor is he dead, for all I know.

HERMIA

I beg you, then, tell me he is all right.

DEMETRIUS

If I could, what would I get in return?

HERMIA

The privilege of never seeing me again.
And from your hated presence, I will depart.   80
Don't try to see me again, whether he is dead or not.

    HERMIA *exits.*

DEMETRIUS

There is no use following her when she is so angry.

Here, therefore, for a while I will remain.
So sorrow's heaviness doth heavier grow
85 For debt that bankrupt sleep doth sorrow owe;
Which now in some slight measure it will pay,
If for his tender here I make some stay.

[DEMETRIUS *lies down and sleeps.*]

OBERON
What hast thou done? Thou hast mistaken quite
And laid the love juice on some true-love's sight.
90 Of thy misprision must perforce ensue
Some true love turn'd and not a false turn'd true.

ROBIN GOODFELLOW
Then fate o'errules, that, one man holding troth,
A million fail, confounding oath on oath.

OBERON
About the wood go swifter than the wind,
95 And Helena of Athens look thou find.
All fancy-sick she is and pale of cheer
With sighs of love, that costs the fresh blood dear.*
By some illusion see thou bring her here.
I'll charm his eyes against she do appear.

ROBIN GOODFELLOW
100 I go, I go, look how I go,
Swifter than arrow from the Tartar's* bow.

[Exit.]

OBERON [*applying the nectar to* DEMETRIUS's *eyes*]
"Flower of this purple dye,
Hit with Cupid's archery,
Sink in apple of his eye.
105 When his love he doth espy,
Let her shine as gloriously
As the Venus of the sky.
When thou wak'st, if she be by,
Beg of her for remedy."

---

97 *With sighs . . . dear.* It was believed that sighs drained blood from the heart.

101 *Tartar* a warrior of a Turkish or Mongolian tribe from Asia

Therefore, I'll stay here for a while.
My sorrow grows heavier
because my sorrow has kept me from sleeping lately.   85
I will now pay back that debt to a slight extent
if I lie down here and offer myself up to sleep.

> (DEMETRIUS *lies down and goes to sleep.*)

OBERON
What have you done? You have made a terrible mistake
and laid the love juice on a true lover's eyes.
Your mistakes have resulted in   90
the estrangement of one true lover and the creation of a true
    lover.

PUCK
Then fate will overrule us. For each man who remains true,
a million will fail and break vow after vow.

OBERON
Go through these woods, swifter than the wind,
and see that you find Helena of Athens.   95
She is lovesick and her face is pale
from sighing, which dangerously saps her blood.
By some magic, see that you bring her here.
I'll charm his eyes in anticipation of her reappearance.

PUCK
I'm going, I'm going! See, I'm off like a shot!   100
Swifter than an arrow from the Tartar's bow.

> *Exit.*

OBERON (*Puts the juice into* DEMETRIUS's *eyes.*)
> *Flower of this purple dye,*
> *Hit him as if aimed by Cupid,*
> *Sink into the apple of his eye.*
> *When he sees his love,*   105
> *Let her shine as gloriously*
> *As Venus in the sky.*
> *When you awake, if she is near,*
> *Beg her for the cure.*

Reenter ROBIN GOODFELLOW.

ROBIN GOODFELLOW

110   "Captain of our fairy band,
    Helena is here at hand;
    And the youth, mistook by me,
    Pleading for a lover's fee.
    Shall we their fond pageant see?
115   Lord, what fools these mortals be!"

OBERON

    "Stand aside. The noise they make
    Will cause Demetrius to awake."

ROBIN GOODFELLOW

    "Then will two at once woo one;
    That must needs be sport alone.
120   And those things do best please me
    That befall preposterously."

Enter LYSANDER *and* HELENA.

LYSANDER

    Why should you think that I should woo in scorn?
    Scorn and **derision** never come in tears.
    Look when I vow, I weep; and vows so born,
125   In their nativity all truth appears.
    How can these things in me seem scorn to you,
    Bearing the badge of faith, to prove them true?

HELENA

    You do advance your cunning more and more.
    When truth kills truth, O devilish holy fray!
130   These vows are Hermia's: will you give her o'er?
    Weigh oath with oath, and you will nothing weigh.
    Your vows to her and me, put in two scales,
    Will even weigh, and both as light as tales.

LYSANDER

    I had no judgment when to her I swore.

PUCK *reenters.*

PUCK

> Captain of our fairy band,   110
> Helena is nearby.
> And the youth I mistakenly daubed with love juice
> Is begging her to love him.
> Shall we watch their silly exhibition?
> Lord, what fools these mortals are!   115

OBERON

> Stand aside. The noise they make
> Will cause Demetrius to wake.

PUCK

> Then the two of them will pursue one girl.
> That will be supreme fun.
> Those things most please me   120
> That are most preposterous.

> LYSANDER *and* HELENA *enter.*

LYSANDER

Why do you think I'm courting you in scorn?
> Scorn and derision are never accompanied by tears.
Look, when I swear to you, I weep. Promises born like that,
> Show themselves completely true from birth.   125
How can these things seem like scorn to you
> When this sign of loyalty proves them to be true?

HELENA

You display your cleverness more and more.
> When truth kills truth, what a terrible battle erupts
> > between true and false!   130
You're giving me the promises you gave to Hermia. Will you
> desert her?
> > If you weigh the one promise with the other, you will have
> > nothing to weigh.
Your vows to her, if you put them on two scales,
Would weigh the same—both are as light as lies.

LYSANDER

I had no judgment when I swore to her.

HELENA

135 Nor none, in my mind, now you give her o'er.

LYSANDER

  Demetrius loves her, and he loves not you.

DEMETRIUS [*waking up*]

  O Helen, goddess, nymph, perfect, divine!
  To what, my love, shall I compare thine eyne?
  Crystal is muddy. O, how ripe in show
140 Thy lips, those kissing cherries, tempting grow!
  That pure **congealed** white, high Taurus's snow,
  Fann'd with the eastern wind, turns to a crow
  When thou hold'st up thy hand. O, let me kiss
  This princess of pure white, this seal of bliss!

HELENA

145 O spite! O hell! I see you all are bent
  To set against me for your merriment.
  If you were civil and knew courtesy,
  You would not do me thus much injury.
  Can you not hate me, as I know you do,
150 But you must join in souls to mock me too?
  If you were men, as men you are in show,
  You would not use a gentle lady so,
  To vow, and swear, and superpraise my parts,
  When I am sure you hate me with your hearts.
155 You both are rivals and love Hermia,
  And now both rivals to mock Helena.
  A trim exploit, a manly enterprise,
  To **conjure** tears up in a poor maid's eyes
  With your derision! None of noble sort
160 Would so offend a virgin and extort
  A poor soul's patience, all to make you sport.

LYSANDER

  You are unkind, Demetrius. Be not so,
  For you love Hermia; this you know I know.

HELENA

And you don't have any, in my opinion, now that you're   135
  throwing her over.

LYSANDER

Demetrius loves her, and he doesn't love you.

DEMETRIUS (*awakening*)

Oh Helen, goddess, nymph, perfect, divine!
To what, my love, shall I compare your eyes?
Crystal is muddy in comparison. Oh, how ripe in appearance
are your lips, like kissing cherries, growing temptations!   140
The pure congealed white of the high Taurus Mountains' snow,
fanned with the eastern winds, turns as black as a crow
when compared to your hand. Oh let me kiss
this princess of pure white, this pledge of bliss!

He reaches for her hand.

HELENA

Oh spiteful men! Oh hell! I see you all are determined   145
to turn against me for your own pleasure.
If you were civilized and had any manners,
you would not hurt me like this.
Can't you just hate me, as I know you do,
without having to scheme together to mock me too?   150
If you were men, as men you appear to be,
you would not mistreat a well-bred lady like this.
You promise and swear and overpraise my qualities
when I am sure you hate me with all your hearts.
You are both rivals, and you love Hermia.   155
Now you're both rivals in mocking me.
It is a wonderful deed, a manly enterprise,
to bring tears to a poor maiden's eyes
with your scorn. No one who was of real nobility
would offend a maiden like this and torture   160
a poor soul's patience, just to entertain you.

LYSANDER

You are unkind, Demetrius. Don't be unkind!
You love Hermia; you know I know that.

And here, with all goodwill, with all my heart,
165   In Hermia's love I yield you up my part;
And yours of Helena to me bequeath,
Whom I do love and will do till my death.

HELENA

Never did mockers waste more idle breath.

DEMETRIUS

Lysander, keep thy Hermia; I will none.
170   If e'er I lov'd her, all that love is gone.
My heart to her but as guest-wise sojourn'd,
And now to Helen is it home return'd,
There to remain.

LYSANDER

                Helen, it is not so.

DEMETRIUS

175   **Disparage** not the faith thou dost not know,
Lest, to thy peril, thou aby it dear.
Look, where thy love comes, yonder is thy dear.

      Reenter HERMIA.

HERMIA

Dark night, that from the eye his function takes,
The ear more quick of apprehension makes;
180   Wherein it doth impair the seeing sense,
It pays the hearing double **recompense.**
Thou art not by mine eye, Lysander, found;
Mine ear, I thank it, brought me to thy sound.
But why unkindly didst thou leave me so?

LYSANDER

185   Why should he stay whom love doth press to go?

HERMIA

What love could press Lysander from my side?

LYSANDER

Lysander's love, that would not let him bide,
Fair Helena, who more engilds the night

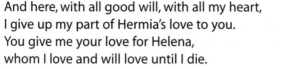

And here, with all good will, with all my heart,
I give up my part of Hermia's love to you.   165
You give me your love for Helena,
whom I love and will love until I die.

HELENA
I have never seen mockers waste such useless breath.

DEMETRIUS
Lysander, keep your Hermia—I don't want any part of her.
If I ever loved her, all that love is gone.   170
My heart merely visited her as a guest,
and now it has returned home to Helena
where it will remain.

LYSANDER
Helena, this is not true.

DEMETRIUS
Don't put down a faith you don't know,   175
or you may pay dearly for it to your regret.
Look, your love is coming. There is your dear one.

>   HERMIA *enters.*

HERMIA (*to* LYSANDER)
Dark night, that makes the eyes useless,
makes the ear quicker to understand.
While it weakens the sense of sight,   180
it makes up for that by doubling the ability to hear.
I did not find you with my eyes, Lysander.
It's thanks to my ears for bringing me to your sound.
But why did you so unkindly leave me like that?

LYSANDER
Why should anyone stay when love urges them to go?   185

HERMIA
What love could urge Lysander to leave me?

LYSANDER
My love, that would not let me stay—
lovely Helena, who decorates the night more

Than all yon fiery oes and eyes of light.*

190 Why seek'st thou me? Could not this make thee know,
The hate I bare thee made me leave thee so?

HERMIA

You speak not as you think. It cannot be.

HELENA

Lo, she is one of this confederacy!
Now I perceive they have conjoin'd all three
195 To fashion this false sport, in spite of me.—
Injurious Hermia! Most ungrateful maid!
Have you conspir'd, have you with these contriv'd
To bait me with this foul derision?
Is all the counsel that we two have shar'd,
200 The sisters' vows, the hours that we have spent
When we have chid the hasty-footed time
For parting us,—O, is all forgot?
All schooldays' friendship, childhood innocence?
We, Hermia, like two artificial gods,
205 Have with our needles created both one flower,
Both on one sampler, sitting on one cushion,
Both warbling of one song, both in one key,
As if our hands, our sides, voices and minds
Had been incorporate. So we grew together,
210 Like to a double cherry, seeming parted,
But yet an union in partition;
Two lovely berries moulded on one stem;
So, with two seeming bodies but one heart;
Two of the first, like coats in heraldry,
215 Due but to one and crowned with one crest.
And will you rend our ancient love asunder,
To join with men in scorning your poor friend?
It is not friendly; 'tis not maidenly.
Our sex, as well as I, may chide you for it,
220 Though I alone do feel the injury.

---

189 *fiery . . . light* Lysander is referring to the stars.

than all those fiery circles and eyes of light.
Why did you seek me out? Doesn't this tell you that the 190
hate I bear toward you made me leave you like that?

HERMIA

You are not saying what you mean. It cannot be.

HELENA

So, she is a part of this plot!
Now I see that all three of them have joined together
to carry out this false game to spite me. 195
Insulting Hermia! You most ungrateful maiden!
Have you conspired, have you plotted with these two
to torture me with this disgusting scorn?
Are all the private conversations that we two shared,
the sisters' vows, the hours we have spent 200
scolding hasty-footed time
for parting us—is all of that forgotten?
Have you forgotten our schoolday friendship and childhood
    innocence?
We, Hermia, like two artistic gods,
have together created one flower with our separate needles 205
on one piece of embroidery, sitting on one cushion,
both singing one song in the same key.
It was as if our hands, our sides, our voices, and our minds,
had been joined in one body. We grew together,
like a double cherry, seemingly separate, 210
yet united even though we were in two parts—
two lovely berries growing from one stem.
In the same way, we seem to have two bodies but one heart.
We are like a shield with two coats of arms
crowned by a single crest. 215
Will you tear our old love apart
to join with these men in scorning your poor friend?
That is not friendly; that is not maidenly!
Apart from me, every other woman could scold you for it,
though I alone have been hurt. 220

HERMIA

I am amazed at your passionate words.
I scorn you not; it seems that you scorn me.

HELENA

Have you not set Lysander, as in scorn,
To follow me and praise my eyes and face?
225 And made your other love, Demetrius,
Who even but now did spurn me with his foot,
To call me goddess, nymph, divine and rare,
Precious, celestial? Wherefore speaks he this
To her he hates? And wherefore doth Lysander
230 Deny your love, so rich within his soul,
And tender me, forsooth, affection,
But by your setting on, by your consent?
What though I be not so in grace as you,
So hung upon with love, so fortunate,
235 But miserable most, to love unlov'd?
This you should pity rather than despise.

HERMIA

I understand not what you mean by this.

HELENA

Ay, do. Persever, counterfeit sad looks,
Make mouths upon me when I turn my back.
240 Wink at each other, hold the sweet jest up;
This sport, well carried, shall be chronicled.
If you have any pity, grace or manners,
You would not make me such an argument.
But fare ye well; 'tis partly my own fault,
245 Which death or absence soon shall remedy.

LYSANDER

Stay, gentle Helena. Hear my excuse,
My love, my life, my soul, fair Helena!

HELENA

O excellent!

HERMIA [*to* LYSANDER]

Sweet, do not scorn her so.

HERMIA

Your passionate words have left me speechless.
I'm not scorning you. I think you're scorning me.

HELENA

Haven't you egged on Lysander to scorn me
by following me and praising my eyes and face?
And didn't you make your other love, Demetrius—   225
who just a while ago spurned me with his foot—
call me goddess, nymph, divine, unique,
precious, and celestial? Why would he say this
to someone he hates? And why does Lysander
deny his love for you—that love which fills his soul—   230
and offer me his affection,
unless you urged him on and agreed to it?
What does it matter if I am not as popular as you are,
or as loved or as fortunate,
instead of being the most miserable and unloved person alive?   235
You should pity me for that reason rather than despise me.

HERMIA

I don't understand what you mean by this.

HELENA

Oh, go ahead! Go on, fake those grave looks,
make faces at me when I turn my back,
wink at each other, keep up the delightful joking.   240
This joke, if you carry it off well, will be legendary.
If you have any pity, goodness, or manners,
you would not make me the subject of such scorn.
But good-bye. This is partly my own fault—
which either my death or my absence will soon remedy.   245

LYSANDER

Stay, noble Helena. Listen to my plea,
my love, my life, my soul, lovely Helena!

HELENA (*sarcastically*)

Oh excellent!

HERMIA (*to* LYSANDER)

My sweet, do not scorn her like that.

DEMETRIUS [*to* LYSANDER]

250   If she cannot entreat, I can compel.

LYSANDER

Thou canst compel no more than she entreat.
Thy threats have no more strength than her weak
        prayers.—
Helen, I love thee. By my life, I do!
255   I swear by that which I will lose for thee,
To prove him false that says I love thee not.

DEMETRIUS

I say I love thee more than he can do.

LYSANDER

If thou say so, withdraw, and prove it too.

DEMETRIUS

Quick, come!

HERMIA

260   Lysander, whereto tends all this?

[*She takes hold of* LYSANDER.]

LYSANDER

Away, you Ethiop!*

DEMETRIUS [*to* HERMIA]

                    No, no. He'll but
Seem to break loose. Take on as you would follow,
But yet come not. You are a tame man, go!

LYSANDER [*to* HERMIA]

265   Hang off, thou cat, thou burr! Vile thing, let loose,
Or I will shake thee from me like a serpent!

HERMIA

Why are you grown so rude? What change is this,
Sweet love?

---

261   *Ethiop* a reference to Hermia's brunette hair

DEMETRIUS

If she can't persuade you, I can force you to stop bothering   250
Helena.

LYSANDER

You can't force me any more than she can persuade me.
Your threats have no more effect on me than her weak prayers.
Helena, I love you. I swear by my life, I do!
I swear by my life, which I would give up for you   255
in order to prove anyone a liar who says I don't love you.

DEMETRIUS

And I say that I love you more than he can.

LYSANDER

If you say that, come with me and prove it.

DEMETRIUS

Let's go right now!

HERMIA

Lysander, what does all of this mean?   260

She grabs him.

LYSANDER

Get away, you dark woman.

He tries to shake her off.

DEMETRIUS (*to* HERMIA)

No, no; he'll
pretend to try to break free and act as if he's upset,
but he won't really leave. (*to* LYSANDER) You are a coward!

LYSANDER (*to* HERMIA)

Let go, you cat, you burr! You vile thing, let go,   265
or I will shake you off like I would a snake!

HERMIA

Why have you grown so rude? What is this change,
my sweet love?

LYSANDER

              Thy love! Out, tawny Tartar, out!
270   Out, loathed med'cine! O hated potion, hence!

HERMIA

Do you not jest?

HELENA

                   Yes, sooth, and so do you.

LYSANDER

Demetrius, I will keep my word with thee.

DEMETRIUS

I would I had your bond, for I perceive
275   A weak bond holds you. I'll not trust your word.

LYSANDER

What, should I hurt her, strike her, kill her dead?
Although I hate her, I'll not harm her so.

HERMIA

What, can you do me greater harm than hate?
Hate me? Wherefore? O me, what news, my love?
280   Am not I Hermia? Are not you Lysander?
I am as fair now as I was erewhile.
Since night you lov'd me; yet since night you left me.
Why, then you left me—O, the gods forbid!—
In earnest, shall I say?

LYSANDER

285   Ay, by my life;
And never did desire to see thee more.
Therefore be out of hope, of question, doubt;
Be certain, nothing truer; 'tis no jest
That I do hate thee and love Helena.

HERMIA

290   O me! [*to* HELENA] You juggler! You canker-blossom!*
You thief of love! What, have you come by night
And stolen my love's heart from him?

---

290   *canker-blossom* probably refers to a worm that destroys the rose blossom

LYSANDER

Your love? Get away, you brown Tartar, away!
Away, you hateful medicine! You hated potion, get away!   270

HERMIA

Surely you're joking?

HELENA

Yes, truly, and so are you.

LYSANDER

Demetrius, I'll keep my promise to fight you.

DEMETRIUS

I wish I had your bond, for I see
that even a weak vow holds you. I won't trust your word.   275

LYSANDER

What do you want me to do? Hurt her, strike her, kill her?
Even though I hate her, I won't harm her like that.

HERMIA

What greater harm can you do me than by hating me?
Hate me? Why? Alas! What is this, my love?
Am I not Hermia? Are you not Lysander?   280
I am as beautiful as I was earlier.
Even up to nightfall you loved me. Yet just since nightfall, you
    left me.
So then, you left me—heaven forbid!—
intentionally? Am I right?

LYSANDER

Yes, yes!   285
And I never wanted to see you again.
Therefore, quit hoping, questioning, and doubting.
You can be certain. There's nothing truer. It's no joke
that I hate you and love Helena. (HERMIA *releases him*)

HERMIA

Alas! (*to* HELENA) You juggler! You worm!   290
You thief of love! So, did you come by night
and steal my love's heart away from him?

HELENA

Fine, i' faith!

Have you no modesty, no maiden shame,

295 No touch of bashfulness? What, will you tear
Impatient answers from my gentle tongue?
Fie, fie! You counterfeit, you puppet, you!

HERMIA

"Puppet?" Why so? Ay, that way goes the game.
Now I perceive that she hath made compare

300 Between our statures; she hath urg'd her height,
And with her personage, her tall personage,
Her height, forsooth, she hath prevail'd with him.
And are you grown so high in his esteem
Because I am so dwarfish and so low?

305 How low am I, thou painted maypole? Speak!
How low am I? I am not yet so low
But that my nails can reach unto thine eyes.

HELENA

I pray you, though you mock me, gentlemen,
Let her not hurt me. I was never curst;

310 I have no gift at all in shrewishness.
I am a right maid for my cowardice.
Let her not strike me. You perhaps may think,
Because she is something lower than myself,
That I can match her.

HERMIA

315 "Lower?" Hark, again.

HELENA

Good Hermia, do not be so bitter with me.
I evermore did love you, Hermia,
Did ever keep your counsels, never wrong'd you—
Save that, in love unto Demetrius,

320 I told him of your stealth unto this wood.
He followed you; for love I followed him.
But he hath chid me hence and threaten'd me
To strike me, spurn me, nay, to kill me too.
And now, so you will let me quiet go,

325 To Athens will I bear my folly back

HELENA

This is fine, indeed!
Don't you have any modesty or shame,
no touch of bashfulness? So, will you tear   295
impatient retorts from my soft-spoken tongue?
For shame! You fake! You puppet, you!

HERMIA

Puppet! Why is that? Oh, so that's the way she wants to play.
Now I see that she's made comparisons
between our heights. She has shown off her height,   300
and with her self, her tall self,
her height, she has won him over.
Have you grown so tall in his esteem
because I am so dwarfish and so short?
How short am I, you painted maypole? Answer me!   305
How short am I? I'm not yet so short
that my nails can't reach your eyes.

HELENA

I beg you, even though you mock me, gentlemen,
don't let her hurt me. I have never been quarrelsome.
I don't have a talent for shrewishness.   310
I am a true young woman in respect to my cowardice.
Don't let her hit me. You perhaps may think
because she is shorter than I am
that I am a match for her.

HERMIA

Shorter! She said it again!   315

HELENA

Good Hermia, don't be so bitter toward me.
I always loved you, Hermia,
always kept your secrets, never did anything to hurt you—
except, out of love for Demetrius,
I told him that you had sneaked into this woods.   320
He followed you. I followed him because I loved him.
But he scolded me to go away and threatened to
strike me, spurn me—yes, even kill me, too.
And now, if you will let me go in peace,
I'll take my foolishness back to Athens,   325

And follow you no further. Let me go.
You see how simple and how fond I am.

HERMIA

Why, get you gone; who is 't that hinders you?

HELENA

A foolish heart, that I leave here behind.

HERMIA

330   What, with Lysander?

HELENA

               With Demetrius.

LYSANDER

Be not afraid; she shall not harm thee, Helena.

DEMETRIUS

No, sir, she shall not, though you take her part.

HELENA

O, when she's angry, she is keen and shrewd.
335   She was a vixen when she went to school,
And though she be but little, she is fierce.

HERMIA

"Little" again? Nothing but "low" and "little"?
Why will you suffer her to flout me thus?
Let me come to her.

LYSANDER

340   Get you gone, you dwarf,
You minimus* of hind'ring knotgrass* made;
You bead, you acorn—

DEMETRIUS

              You are too officious
In her behalf that scorns your services.
345   Let her alone; speak not of Helena;
Take not her part; for, if thou dost intend
Never so little show of love to her,
Thou shalt aby it.

---

341   *minimus* the smallest of creatures

341   *knotgrass* supposedly stunted one's growth

and follow you no more. Let me go.
You see how simple-minded and foolish I am.

HERMIA

Well then, go! Who's stopping you?

HELENA

My foolish heart which I leave behind here.

HERMIA

With Lysander? 330

HELENA

With Demetrius.

LYSANDER

Don't be afraid. She shall not harm you, Helena.

DEMETRIUS

No, sir, she shall not, even though you offer to be her defender.

HELENA

Oh, when she's angry, she's cruel and shrewish.
She was a terror when she went to school. 335
And though she's small, she's fierce.

HERMIA

"Small" again! Again and again "short" and "small!"
Why do you let her insult me like this?
Let me at her!

LYSANDER

Go away, you dwarf! 340
You must have been fed on knotgrass, you worm!
You bead, you acorn!

DEMETRIUS

You are overly concerned
about defending someone who scorns your help.
Leave her alone. Don't talk about Helena. 345
Don't take her side. If you offer
even a little show of love for her,
you'll regret it.

LYSANDER

                  Now she holds me not.
350   Now follow, if thou dar'st, to try whose right,
Of thine or mine, is most in Helena.

DEMETRIUS

"Follow"? Nay, I'll go with thee, cheek by jowl.

[*Exeunt* LYSANDER *and* DEMETRIUS.]

HERMIA

You, mistress, all this coil is long of you.
Nay, go not back.

HELENA

                  I will not trust you, I,
355   Nor longer stay in your curst company.
Your hands than mine are quicker for a fray;
My legs are longer though, to run away.

[*Exit.*]

HERMIA

I am amaz'd and know not what to say.

[*Exit.*]

OBERON

360   This is thy negligence. Still thou mistak'st,
Or else committ'st thy knaveries willfully.

ROBIN GOODFELLOW

Believe me, king of shadows, I mistook.
Did not you tell me I should know the man
By the Athenian garments he had on?
365   And so far blameless proves my enterprise,
That I have 'nointed an Athenian's eyes;
And so far am I glad it did sort,
As this their jangling I esteem a sport.

OBERON

Thou see'st these lovers seek a place to fight;
370   Hie therefore, Robin, overcast the night.
The starry welkin cover thou anon

LYSANDER

Hermia isn't holding me back now.

So follow me, now, if you dare. We'll see who most deserves   350

Helena—you or me.

DEMETRIUS

Follow? No, I'll go with you, side by side.

> LYSANDER *and* DEMETRIUS *exit.*

HERMIA

You, woman, you are the cause of all this trouble. (HELENA *backs up.*)

—No, don't go back.

HELENA

I don't trust you,   355

nor will I stay any longer in your cruel company.

Your hands are quicker than mine for a fight;

but my legs are longer for running away.

> HELENA *exits.*

HERMIA

I am confused and don't know what to say.

> HERMIA *exits.*

OBERON (*to* PUCK)

This is all your fault. You're still confusing things   360

or else making this mischief on purpose.

PUCK

Believe me, king of shadows, it was an accident.

Didn't you tell me I should recognize the man

by the Athenian garments he had on?

You see that I am innocent in the way I did my duty   365

because I did anoint an Athenian's eyes.

And I'm glad it turned out this way

because I think their fighting is entertaining.

OBERON

You heard that these lovers are looking for a place to fight.

Therefore, run, Robin, make the night overcast.   370

Cover the starry sky at once

With drooping fog as black as Acheron,*
And lead these testy rivals so astray
As one come not within another's way.

375 Like to Lysander sometime frame thy tongue;
Then stir Demetrius up with bitter wrong.
And sometime rail thou like Demetrius.
And from each other look thou lead them thus,
Till o'er their brows death-counterfeiting sleep
380 With leaden legs and batty wings doth creep.
Then crush this herb into Lysander's eye;

[*He gives the flower to* ROBIN.]

Whose liquor hath this virtuous property,
To take from thence all error with his might
And make his eyeballs roll with wonted sight.
385 When they next wake, all this derision
Shall seem a dream and fruitless vision.
And back to Athens shall the lovers wend,
With league whose date till death shall never end.
Whiles I in this affair do thee employ,
390 I'll to my queen and beg her Indian boy;
And then I will her charmed eye release
From monster's view, and all things shall be peace.

ROBIN GOODFELLOW
My fairy lord, this must be done with haste,
For night's swift dragons cut the clouds full fast,
395 And yonder shines Aurora's* harbinger,
At whose approach, ghosts, wand'ring here and there,
Troop home to churchyards. Damned spirits all,
That in crossways and floods* have burial,
Already to their wormy beds are gone.
400 For fear lest day should look their shames upon,
They willfully themselves exile from light
And must for aye consort with black-brow'd night.

---

372 *Acheron* a river in Hades, the world of the dead in classical mythology

395 *Aurora* the goddess of the dawn

397–98 *Damned . . . floods* those who had been buried without holy ceremonies.
Suicides were buried at crossroads without church rites because suicide was
considered a crime. Drowning victims whose bodies were not recovered were
believed to roam the earth because they had not been properly buried.

with drooping fog, as black as the Acheron.
Lead these angry rivals so far apart
that the one will not come near the other.
Imitate Lysander's voice sometimes,   375
and make Demetrius angry with bitter insults.
Then sometimes yell like Demetrius.
Be sure to lead them apart like this
until deathlike sleep comes creeping
over their eyes with heavy legs and batlike wings.   380
Then crush this herb into Lysander's eyes.

    He gives the flower to PUCK.

Its juice has the valuable quality
of removing all delusions with its power.
It will make his eyes function with their normal sight.
When they awake again, all this foolishness   385
will seem like a dream and an unreal vision.
Then back to Athens the lovers will go,
united in love until death.
While you are taking care of this,
I'll go to my queen and ask her for the Indian boy.   390
And then I will clear her enchanted eyes
of her monstrous delusion, and everything will be peaceful.

PUCK
My fairy lord, this must be done quickly,
for night's swift dragons are swiftly moving through the sky,
and over there, the morning star is shining,   395
at whose approach, ghosts, wandering here and there,
troop home to churchyards. All of the damned spirits
that are buried in the crossroads and water
have already gone to their wormy graves
because they do not want the daylight to see their shame. 400
So, they willfully exile themselves from light
and must forever associate with black-browed night.

OBERON
But we are spirits of another sort.
I with the Morning's love* have oft made sport,
405   And, like a forester, the groves may tread
Even till the eastern gate, all fiery-red,
Opening on Neptune with fair blessed beams,
Turns into yellow gold his salt-green streams.
But, notwithstanding, haste! Make no delay.
410   We may effect this business yet ere day.

       [*Exit.*]

ROBIN GOODFELLOW
"Up and down, up and down,
I will lead them up and down.
I am fear'd in field and town.
Goblin, lead them up and down."
415   Here comes one.

       Enter LYSANDER.

LYSANDER
Where art thou, proud Demetrius? Speak thou now.

ROBIN GOODFELLOW [*in* DEMETRIUS's *voice*]
Here, villain, drawn and ready. Where are thou?

LYSANDER
I will be with thee straight.

ROBIN GOODFELLOW [*in* DEMETRIUS's *voice*]
Follow me, then, to plainer ground.

       [*Exit* LYSANDER, *as following the voice.*]

       Enter DEMETRIUS.

DEMETRIUS
420   Lysander, speak again!
Thou runaway, thou coward, art thou fled?
Speak! In some bush? Where dost thou hide thy head?

ROBIN GOODFELLOW [*in* LYSANDER's *voice*]
Thou coward, art thou bragging to the stars,

---

404 *Morning's love* either Aurora or her lover, Cephalus

OBERON

But we are spirits of another sort.
I have often romped with Morning's love.
Like a forester, I walk through the groves   405
until the sun in the eastern sky, all fiery red,
dawns upon the sea with beautiful blessed beams,
turning the sea's salty green streams to yellow gold.
But hurry now. Do not delay.
We may get this business done yet before day.   410

     OBERON exits.

PUCK

Up and down, up and down,
I will lead them up and down.
I am feared in field and town.
I, Hobgoblin, will lead them up and down.
Here comes one of them.   415

     LYSANDER enters.

LYSANDER

Where are you, proud Demetrius? Say something!

PUCK (*imitating* DEMETRIUS)

Here I am, villain. My sword is drawn and ready. Where are you?

LYSANDER

I'm right behind you.

PUCK (*imitating* DEMETRIUS)

Follow me, then, to more level ground.

     LYSANDER exits.

     DEMETRIUS enters.

DEMETRIUS

Lysander, say something again!   420
You runaway, you coward, have you fled?
Speak! Are you in a bush? Where are you hiding?

PUCK (*imitating* LYSANDER)

You coward, are you bragging to the stars,

425 Telling the bushes that thou look'st for wars,
And wilt not come? Come, recreant! Come, thou child,
I'll whip thee with a rod. He is defil'd
That draws a sword on thee.*

DEMETRIUS
Yea, art thou there?

ROBIN GOODFELLOW [*in* LYSANDER's *voice*]
Follow my voice. We'll try no manhood here.

[*Exeunt.*]

Reenter LYSANDER.

LYSANDER
430 He goes before me and still dares me on.
When I come where he calls, then he is gone.
The villain is much lighter-heel'd than I.
I followed fast, but faster he did fly,
Than fallen am I in dark uneven way,
435 And here will rest me. Come, thou gentle day!

[*Lies down.*]

For if but once thou show me thy gray light,
I'll find Demetrius and revenge this spite.

[*Sleeps.*]

Reenter ROBIN GOODFELLOW *and* DEMETRIUS.

ROBIN GOODFELLOW [*in* LYSANDER's *voice*]
Ho, ho, ho! Coward, why com'st thou not?

DEMETRIUS
Abide me, if thou dar'st; for well I wot
440 Thou runn'st before me, shifting every place,
And dar'st not stand, nor look me in the face.
Where are thou now?

ROBIN GOODFELLOW [*in* LYSANDER's *voice*]
Come hither. I am here.

426–427 *I'll . . . sword* Puck's taunt implies that it would be unfair to attack a "child"
like Demetrius with an adult weapon such as a sword. The only fitting
punishment for him would be a spanking.

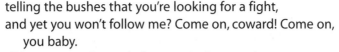

telling the bushes that you're looking for a fight,
and yet you won't follow me? Come on, coward! Come on,   425
    you baby.
I'll beat you with a rod. The man is disgraced
who would fight you with a sword.

DEMETRIUS
So, are you there?

PUCK (*imitating* LYSANDER)
Follow the sound of my voice. We won't test our bravery here.

ALL *exit*.

LYSANDER *enters*.

LYSANDER
He's ahead of me, always daring me to follow.   430
When I go where he calls, he's already gone.
The villain is much faster than I am.
I followed him quickly, but he ran even more quickly,
so that I have stumbled into this dark, rough place.
And here I will rest. Come, you gentle day!   435

He lies down.

If just once you'll show me your gray light,
I'll find Demetrius and get revenge for this insult.

LYSANDER *goes to sleep*.

PUCK *and* DEMETRIUS *enter*.

PUCK (*imitating* LYSANDER)
Ho, ho, ho! Coward, why aren't you following me?

DEMETRIUS
Wait for me, if you dare, for I'm sure
that you are running before me, darting from place to place,   440
and not daring to stand still or look me in the face.
Where are you now?

PUCK (*imitating* LYSANDER)
Come here. I am here.

DEMETRIUS

Nay, then, thou mock'st me. Thou shalt buy this dear,
445   If ever I thy face by daylight see.
Now, go thy way. Faintness constraineth me
To measure out my length on this cold bed.
By day's approach look to be visited.

[Lies down and sleeps.]

Enter HELENA.

HELENA

O weary night, O long and tedious night,
450   **Abate** thy hours! Shine, comforts, from the east,
That I may back to Athens by daylight
    From these that my poor company detest.
And sleep, that sometimes shuts up sorrow's eye,
Steal me awhile from mine own company.

[Lies down and sleeps.]

ROBIN GOODFELLOW

455   "Yet but three? Come one more;
Two of both kinds makes up four.
Here she comes, curst and sad.
Cupid is a knavish lad,
Thus to make poor females mad."

Reenter Hermia.

HERMIA

460   Never so weary, never so in woe,
    Bedabbled with the dew and torn with briers,
I can no further crawl, no further go.
    My legs can keep no pace with my desires.
Here will I rest me till the break of day.
465   Heavens shield Lysander, if they mean a fray!

[Lies down and sleeps.]

ROBIN GOODFELLOW

"On the ground
Sleep sound.
I'll apply
To your eye,

DEMETRIUS

I see; you're mocking me. You'll pay for this dearly
if I ever see your face by daylight.   445
Now, go away. Exhaustion forces me
to stretch out on this cold ground.
You can be sure I'll find you when daylight comes.

> DEMETRIUS *lies down and goes to sleep.*

> HELENA *enters.*

HELENA

Oh weary night, oh long and tedious night,
> Cut short your hours! Shine some comfort from the east   450
So I can get back to Athens by daylight,
> Away from these people who detest me.
Sleep, that sometimes shuts up sorrow's eyes,
Please take me away for a while from my own company.

> HELENA *sleeps.*

PUCK

> Still only three of them? I need one more.   455
> Two of both sexes make up four.
> Here she comes, cross and sad.
> Cupid is a wicked lad
> to make poor females mad like this.

> HERMIA *enters.*

HERMIA

I have never been so tired or so sad.   460
> I am wet with dew and torn by thorns.
I can't crawl any further or go any further.
> My legs can't keep pace with my desires.
I will rest here until morning.
May the heavens protect Lysander, if he means to fight.   465

> HERMIA *lies down and goes to sleep.*

PUCK

> *On the ground*
> *Sleep sound.*
> *I'll apply*
> *To your eye,*

470   Gentle lover, remedy."

    [*Squeezes the juice on Lysander's eyes.*]

        "When thou wak'st,
        Thou tak'st
        True delight
        In the sight
475   Of thy former lady's eye.
    And the country proverb known,
    That every man should take his own,
    In your waking shall be shown.
        Jack shall have Jill;
480   Nought shall go ill;
    The man shall have his mare again, and all shall
      be well."

    [*Exit.*]

Gentle lover, a remedy. 470

(*He squeezes the juice on* LYSANDER's *eyelids.*)

When you wake,
You'll take
True delight
In the sight
Of your former lady-love's eyes. 475
And the well-known country proverb,
that every man must take his own,
will be proven when you awaken.
Jack will have his Jill.
Nothing will go ill. 480
The man will have his mare again, and all will be well.

PUCK *exits.*

Act III Review

Discussion Questions

1. As the actors rehearse, they encounter several problems to be solved. What are those problems, and how do they deal with them?

2. From the attitude and actions of the workmen/actors in this act, do you think Shakespeare treats them with respect, condescension, or a little of both? Explain your response with examples from the text.

3. Most readers or audience members think the workmen/ actors in this act provide comic relief. What do you think the fairies provide?

4. Bottom makes the comment that "reason and love keep little company together nowadays" (Scene i, lines 124–125). Explain what you think this means and whether or not you agree.

5. There are several transformations in this act, one being when Puck transforms Bottom's head into an ass's head. Identify some of the other transformations, and explain how they contribute to the ideas and themes of the play.

6. Some readers and audience members find the fairies in this comedy delightful; others find them silly and annoying. Discuss your own reaction to them.

Literary Questions

1. Good drama has **conflict**: struggle between opposing forces and desires. Several conflicts must be resolved before the play is over. Identify one of them, and describe how you would resolve it in the next two acts.

2. What makes Scene ii, where the lovers confront each other, **comical**?

3. What **genres** of literature—fairy tale, romance, or others—can you identify so far in the play? Pinpoint the scene or lines that represent each genre.

Writing Prompts

1. Reread the exchanges between Titania and Bottom in Scene i, considering what makes them comical. Now rewrite the couple's exchanges in hip, contemporary language.

2. Imagine that the scenes of Act III are episodes of an ongoing daily soap opera. In contemporary language, write newspaper synopses for fans that have missed the episodes based on each scene.

3. Using a chart, describe and give examples of the dialogue of the workmen, the fairies, and the young lovers. Now write a brief essay analyzing how their dialogue may differ and how this develops the plot and characters.

4. The word *puckish*, named after the character of Puck, came into the language after this play was first performed. This made it a *neologism*, or a newly coined word. From your knowledge of Puck, write a definition of the adjective *puckish*. Then look it up in the dictionary to see how close you came.

A Midsummer Night's Dream

ACT IV

Christopher Lloyd as Oberon and Carmen de Lavallade as Titania at the Yale Repertory Theatre

*"Methought I was
enamour'd of an ass."*

Before You Read

1. What response do you think Bottom will have when Titania suddenly falls out of love with him?

2. In the act you are about to read, Lysander will once again love Hermia. She doesn't know that he fell out of love with her and then back in again because of the magic potions. How do you think she might respond to his sudden changes of heart?

3. The characters of Helena, Puck, and Oberon are all sometimes manipulative. Do you think it is ever fair to control another person to your own advantage? Explain your answer.

4. Dreams continue to be very important in this play. What purposes do you think dreaming serves?

Literary Elements

1. **Hyperbole** means exaggeration used for effect. In Act III, Titania uses heightened language to describe her feelings when she first glimpses Bottom, for example, "So is mine eye enthralled to thy shape . . . ."

2. Writers create **contrast** when they show something against its opposite to highlight the differences. In this play, what happens during the day contrasts with what happens during the night.

3. A **symbol** is an object, person, place, or thing that stands for something else. In Act I, Theseus uses a rose as a symbol for a young woman, saying that the rose picked for perfume (chosen by a husband) is happier than the rose that stays on the vine.

4. **Similes** are comparisons between unlike things that use *like* or *as*. A **metaphor** makes a direct comparison between unlike things that nevertheless have something in common. In Act II, when Helena says to Demetrius "I am your spaniel," she is speaking metaphorically—suggesting that she will be as good-natured and obedient as this gentle breed of dog.

Words to Know

The following vocabulary words appear in Act IV in the original text of Shakespeare's play. However, they are words that are still used today. Read the definitions here and pay attention to the words as you read the play (they will be in boldfaced type).

amiable	friendly; likeable
amity	friendship; love
conjunction	together; in combination
discourse	talk; conversation
dotage	feeble-mindedness; delusionment
enmity	harm; ill will
jollity	good cheer; merriment
paragon	model of excellence; shining example
recount	tell; relate
visage	face; countenance

Act Summary

As the four young lovers sleep, King Oberon tells Puck that when he came upon Titania earlier, she was so obsessed with Bottom that she agreed to let the king have the boy they had quarreled over as his attendant. Having gotten what he wanted, Oberon instructs Puck to take the ass's head off of Bottom while he removes the spell from his queen.

Theseus, the duke who is about to be married, and Egeus, the father of Hermia, leave Athens to go into the forest and tell hunters to awaken Lysander, Demetrius, Hermia, and Helena with their horns. Upon awakening, the young people are so foggy about the recent events brought on by the spells that they conclude they have been dreaming. The two couples pair off—Lysander with Hermia, Demetrius with Helena. Oberon reunites with Titania. Bottom returns to the troupe of actors, who are rehearsing the play in Athens.

When Theseus sees that all of the young people are happy, he overrules Egeus's ultimatum to Hermia to marry Demetrius and proclaims that both couples shall be married in a triple wedding ceremony with him and Hippolyta. Bottom returns to the troupe of actors, who are rehearsing the play in Athens.

Puck, the Indian boy, and Oberon, 1982 production at the Delacorte Theatre in Central Park

ACT IV, SCENE I

[*The same.*] LYSANDER, DEMETRIUS, HELENA, *and*
HERMIA, *lying asleep. Enter* TITANIA *and clown*
BOTTOM; PEASEBLOSSOM, COBWEB, MOTH,
MUSTARDSEED, *and other* FAIRIES *attending;*
OBERON *behind, unseen.*

TITANIA [*to* BOTTOM]
Come, sit thee down upon this flow'ry bed,
    While I thy **amiable** cheeks do coy,
And stick muskroses in thy sleek smooth head,
    And kiss thy fair large ears, my gentle joy.

BOTTOM
5   Where's Peaseblossom?

PEASEBLOSSOM
Ready.

BOTTOM
Scratch my head, Peaseblossom. Where's Monsieur Cobweb?

COBWEB
Ready.

BOTTOM
Monsieur Cobweb, good monsieur, get you your weapon
10   in your hand, and kill me a red-hipp'd humble-bee on the
top of a thistle; and, good monsieur, bring me the honey-
bag. Do not fret yourself too much in the action,
monsieur, and, good monsieur, have a care the honey-bag
break not; I would be loath to have you overflown with a
15   honey-bag, signior. [COBWEB *exits.*] Where's Monsieur
Mustardseed?

MUSTARDSEED
Ready.

BOTTOM
Give me your neaf, Monsieur Mustardseed. Pray you, leave
your courtesy, good monsieur.

MUSTARDSEED
20   What's your will?

ACT 4, SCENE 1

The woods. LYSANDER, DEMETRIUS, HELENA, *and* HERMIA *are lying asleep.* TITANIA, BOTTOM, *the clown,* PEASEBLOSSOM, COBWEB, MOTH, MUSTARDSEED, *and other* FAIRIES *enter.* OBERON *enters behind the rest, unseen.*

TITANIA (*to* BOTTOM)
Come, sit down upon this flowery bed
    While I stroke your lovely cheeks
And stick musk roses in your sleek, smooth head
    And kiss your beautiful, large ears, my noble love.

BOTTOM
Where's Peaseblossom?   5

PEASEBLOSSOM
At your service.

BOTTOM
Scratch my head, Peaseblossom. Where's Mr. Cobweb?

COBWEB
At your service.

BOTTOM
Mr. Cobweb, good sir, get your weapons and kill me a
red-hipped bumblebee on top of a thistle. And good sir,   10
bring me the honey bag. Don't exert yourself too much doing
this, sir. And, good sir, be careful that the honey bag does not
break. I would hate to have you drenched in honey, sir.   15
(COBWEB *exits.*) Where's Mr. Mustardseed?

MUSTARDSEED
At your service.

BOTTOM
Give me your hand, Mr. Mustardseed. Please stop bowing, good sir.

MUSTARDSEED
What do you wish?   20

BOTTOM

Nothing, good monsieur, but to help Cavalery Cobweb to scratch. I must to the barber's, monsieur; for methinks I am marvels hairy about the face; and I am such a tender ass, if my hair do but tickle me, I must scratch.

TITANIA

25 What, wilt thou hear some music, my sweet love?

BOTTOM

I have a reasonable good ear in music. Let's have the tongs and the bones.*

[*Music. Tongs. Rural music.*]

TITANIA

Or say, sweet love, what thou desir'st to eat.

BOTTOM

Truly, a peck of provender; I could munch your good dry
30 oats. Methinks I have a great desire to a bottle of hay. Good hay, sweet hay, hath no fellow.

TITANIA

I have a venturous fairy that shall seek
The squirrel's hoard and fetch for thee new nuts.

BOTTOM

I had rather have a handful or two of dried peas. But, I
35 pray you, let none of your people stir me; I have an exposition* of sleep come upon me.

TITANIA

Sleep thou, and I will wind thee in my arms.—
Fairies, be gone, and be always away.

[*Exeunt* FAIRIES.]

So doth the woodbine the sweet honeysuckle
40 Gently entwist; the female ivy* so
Enrings the barky fingers of the elm.
O, how I love thee! How I dote on thee!

[*They sleep.*]

26–27 *tongs and the bones* crude musical instruments of the time

36 *exposition* Bottom's malapropism for "disposition"

40 *female ivy* depends upon the tree for support like a wife was supposed to depend upon her husband

BOTTOM

Nothing, good sir, except that you help Cavalier Cobweb to scratch me. I must go to the barber, sir, for I think I am amazingly hairy about the face. And I'm such a tender ass that if my hair tickles me, I have to scratch.

TITANIA

Would you like to hear some music, my sweet love?   25

BOTTOM

I have a reasonably good ear for music. Let's hear the tongs and the bones.

Music is played.

TITANIA

Tell me, my sweet love, what would you like to eat?

BOTTOM

Really, I'd like a peck of dry food. I could munch some good, dry oats. I think I really feel like having a bundle of hay. Good hay,   30
sweet hay, has no equal.

TITANIA

I have an adventurous fairy that will find
a squirrel's storehouse and get you some nuts.

BOTTOM

I'd rather have a handful or two of dried peas. But, I beg you, don't let any of your people bother me. I have an   35
exposition for sleep now.

TITANIA

Sleep, and I will fold you in my arms.
Fairies, go away. Spread out in every direction.

The FAIRIES *exit.*

TITANIA *hugs* BOTTOM.

In just this way the woodbine wraps around the honeysuckle
gently. Just like this, the clinging ivy   40
encircles the bark on the branches of the elm.
Oh, how I love you! How I adore you!

They go to sleep.

Enter ROBIN GOODFELLOW.

OBERON [*advancing*]
    Welcome, good Robin. See'st thou this sweet sight?
    Her **dotage** now I do begin to pity.
45   For, meeting her of late behind the wood,
    Seeking sweet favours for this hateful fool,
    I did upbraid her and fall out with her.
    For she his hairy temples then had rounded
    With coronet of fresh and fragrant flowers;
50   And that same dew, which sometime on the buds
    Was wont to swell like round and orient pearls,
    Stood now within the pretty flowerets' eyes
    Like tears that did their own disgrace bewail.
    When I had at my pleasure taunted her,
55   And she in mild terms begg'd my patience,
    I then did ask of her her changeling child;
    Which straight she gave me, and her fairy sent
    To bear him to my bower in Fairyland.
    And now I have the boy, I will undo
60   This hateful imperfection of her eyes.
    And, gentle Puck, take this transformed scalp
    From off the head of this Athenian swain,
    That, he awaking when the other do,
    May all to Athens back again repair
65   And think no more of this night's accidents
    But as the fierce vexation of a dream.
    But first I will release the Fairy Queen.

        [*Touching her eyes.*]

    "Be as thou wast wont to be;
    See as thou wast wont to see.
70   Dian's bud* o'er Cupid's flower
    Hath such force and blessed power."
    Now, my Titania; wake you, my sweet queen.

TITANIA [*waking*]
    My Oberon! What visions have I seen!
    Methought I was enamour'd of an ass.

---

70 *Dian's bud* a flower from a special tree believed to keep one as chaste as the
virgin goddess Diana

PUCK *enters.*

OBERON (*coming forward*)
Welcome, good Robin. Do you see this sweet sight?
I'm beginning to pity her delusionment.
I met her recently behind the woods   45
as she was searching for sweet love tokens for this hateful fool.
I scolded her and quarreled with her.
She had covered his hairy forehead
with a crown of fresh and fragrant flowers,
and the dew, which once on the flower's buds   50
used to swell like round and glowing pearls,
now filled the pretty flowerlets' eyes
like tears that cried over their own disgrace.
After I had teased her to my heart's content,
she gently begged me to be patient.   55
Then I asked her for her changeling child,
and she immediately gave him to me, sending her fairy
to take him to my chamber in fairyland.
Now that I have the boy, I will remove
this hateful error in her vision.   60
And you, gentle Puck, remove this ass's head
from the head of this Athenian lover
so that when he awakes at the same time as the others,
they can all go back to Athens,
and think no more about the events of this night   65
except as the disturbance of a bad dream.
But first I will release the fairy queen.

    (*to* TITANIA)

Be as you used to be.
See as you used to see.
Over Cupid's flower, Diana's flower   70
Has force and blessed power.
Now, my Titania, awake, my sweet queen!

TITANIA (*waking*)
My Oberon, I have dreamed such strange things!
I thought I was in love with an ass.

OBERON

75   There lies your love.

TITANIA

How came these things to pass?
O, how mine eyes do loathe his **visage** now!

OBERON

Silence awhile.—Robin, take off this head.—
Titania, music call; and strike more dead
80   Than common sleep of all these five the sense.

TITANIA

Music, ho, music, such as charmeth sleep!

[*Music, still.*]

ROBIN GOODFELLOW [*removing the ass-head from* BOTTOM]
Now, when thou wak'st, with thine own fool's eyes peep.

OBERON

Sound, music!

Come, my queen, take hands with me,
85   And rock the ground whereon these sleepers be.

[TITANIA *and* OBERON *dance.*]

Now thou and I are new in **amity**
And will tomorrow midnight solemnly
Dance in Duke Theseus's house triumphantly,
And bless it to all fair prosperity.
90   There shall the pairs of faithful lovers be
Wedded, with Theseus, all in **jollity**.

ROBIN GOODFELLOW

"Fairy King, attend and mark;
I do hear the morning lark."

OBERON

"Then, my queen, in silence sad
95   Trip we after the night's shade.
We the globe can compass soon,
Swifter than the wand'ring moon."

TITANIA

"Come, my lord, and in our flight

OBERON

There lies your love. 75

TITANIA

How did this happen?
Oh, how my eyes hate his face now.

OBERON

Be quiet now. Robin, take off this ass's head.
Titania, call for music and put these five
into an uncommonly deep sleep. 80

TITANIA

Music! Bring music! Music that will charm them to sleep!

Music is played.

PUCK (*Removes ass-head from* BOTTOM.)
Now when you awake, see with your own foolish eyes.

OBERON

Sound the music! Come, my queen, join hands,
and we'll rock the ground where these sleepers lie. 85

They dance.

Now you and I are renewed in love,
and tomorrow night, we will ceremoniously
dance in Duke Theseus's house in all our glory,
and give them our blessings for a happy future.
There the pairs of faithful lovers will be 90
wedded, along with Theseus, in great merriment.

PUCK

Fairy King, listen.
I hear the morning lark.

OBERON

Then, my queen, with serious ceremony,
We'll follow the night, stepping light. 95
We can circle the world in a twinkling,
Swifter than the wandering moon.

TITANIA

Come, my lord, and during our flight,
Tell me how it came about tonight

Tell me how it came this night
100   That I sleeping here was found
With these mortals on the ground."

[*Exeunt. Horns winded within.*]

Enter THESEUS *and all this* TRAIN, HIPPOLYTA, *and*
EGEUS.

THESEUS
Go, one of you, find out the Forester.
For now our observation is perform'd,
And, since we have the vaward of the day,
105   My love shall hear the music of my hounds.
Uncouple in the western valley, let them go.
Dispatch, I say, and find the Forester.

[*Exit an* ATTENDANT.]

We will, fair queen, up to the mountain's top
And mark the musical confusion
110   Of hounds and echo in **conjunction**.

HIPPOLYTA
I was with Hercules and Cadmus* once,
When in a wood of Crete they bay'd the bear
With hounds of Sparta. Never did I hear
Such gallant chiding, for, besides the groves,
115   The skies, the fountains, every region near
Seem'd all one mutual cry. I never heard
So musical a discord, such sweet thunder.

THESEUS
My hounds are bred out of the Spartan kind,
So flew'd, so sanded, and their heads are hung
120   With ears that sweep away the morning dew;
Crook-knee'd, and dewlapp'd like Thessalian bulls;
Slow in pursuit, but match'd in mouth like bells,
Each under each. A cry more tunable
Was never holloed to, nor cheer'd with horn,
125   In Crete, in Sparta, nor in Thessaly.*
Judge when you hear.—But, soft! What nymphs are these?

---

111   *Hercules and Cadmus* two heroes of Greek mythology

125   *Thessaly* a large area of ancient Greece

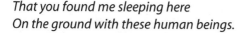

That you found me sleeping here   100
On the ground with these human beings.

(*They exit.*)

(*A horn is heard and* THESEUS *enters with* HIPPOLYTA, EGEUS,
and all of his TRAIN.)

THESEUS

Go, one of you, find the Forester.
For now we've performed our May Day rites.
And since the day is just beginning,
you, my love, will hear the music of my hounds.   105
Let them loose in the western valley; let them go.
Go, I say, and find the Forester.

   An ATTENDANT *exits.*

Beautiful queen, we will go up to the mountain top,
and listen to the musical confusion of the sounds
of hounds and echoes mixed together.   110

HIPPOLYTA

I was with Hercules and Cadmus once
when in a wood of Crete they cornered a bear
with Spartan dogs. I have never heard
such loud yowling. Besides the woods,
the skies, the fountains, and every place nearby   115
seemed to be ringing with the same sound. I never heard
such musical clamoring, such sweet thunder.

THESEUS

My hounds are bred from the Spartan breed.
They have the same sagging cheeks, the sandy color, and they have
ears so low that they sweep the dewy ground.   120
They have bent knees, and they have dewlaps like Thessalian bulls.
They are slow in pursuit, but their voices are matched like bells
of different tones. A more tuneful pack of hounds
was never yelled to or cheered with horns,
in Crete, in Sparta, or in Thessaly.   125
Judge for yourself when you hear. But, stop! Who are these nymphs?

EGEUS

My lord, this is my daughter here asleep;
And this, Lysander; this Demetrius is;
This Helena, old Nedar's Helena.
130   I wonder of their being here together.

THESEUS

No doubt they rose up early to observe
The rite of May, and hearing our intent,
Came here in grace of our solemnity.
But speak, Egeus. Is not this the day
135   That Hermia should give answer of her choice?

EGEUS

It is, my lord.

THESEUS

Go, bid the huntsmen wake them with their horns.

[*Horns and shout within. LYSANDER, DEMETRIUS,*
HELENA, and HERMIA wake and start up.]

Good morrow, friends. Saint Valentine is past.
Begin these woodbirds but to couple now?*

[*The LOVERS kneel.*]

LYSANDER

140   Pardon, my lord.

THESEUS

                              I pray you all, stand up.
I know you two are rival enemies;
How comes this gentle concord in the world,
That hatred is so far from jealousy
145   To sleep by hate and fear no **enmity**?

LYSANDER

My lord, I shall reply amazedly,
Half sleep, half waking; but as yet, I swear,
I cannot truly say how I came here.

138–39 *Saint Valentine . . . now?* Birds supposedly began mating on St. Valentine's
Day, February 14.

EGEUS

My lord, this is my daughter here asleep.
And this is Lysander. This is Demetrius.
This is Helena—old Nedar's Helena.
I wonder why they are here together.   130

THESEUS

No doubt they arose early to perform
the May Day rites, and hearing of our plans,
they came here to honor our ceremony.
But tell me, Egeus, isn't this the day
that Hermia must announce her choice?   135

EGEUS

It is, my lord.

THESEUS

Go, tell the hunters to wake them with their horns.

> *A shout is heard offstage. Horns sound. The lovers all wake up.*

Good morning, friends. Saint Valentine is past.
Are these birds just starting to mate at this late date?

> *The LOVERS kneel.*

LYSANDER

I beg your pardon, my lord.   140

THESEUS

I beg you all, stand up.
I know you two young men are rivals in love,
so how does it happen that you are so at peace,
and your hatred is so far removed from suspicion
that you can sleep by one you hate and fear no harm?   145

LYSANDER

My lord, I will give you a confused reply
since I am half asleep and half awake. But right now, I swear,
I cannot truthfully say how I got here.

But, as I think—for truly would I speak,
150 And now I do bethink me, so it is:
I came with Hermia hither. Our intent
Was to be gone from Athens, where we might,
Without the peril of the Athenian law—

EGEUS

Enough, enough!—My lord; you have enough.
155 I beg the law, the law, upon his head.
They would have stol'n away.—They would, Demetrius,
Thereby to have defeated you and me:
You of your wife and me of my consent,
Of my consent that she should be your wife.

DEMETRIUS

160 My lord, fair Helen told me of their stealth,
Of this their purpose hither to this wood,
And I in fury hither follow'd them,
Fair Helena in fancy following me.
But, my good lord, I wot not by what power—
165 But by some power it is—my love to Hermia,
Melted as is the snow, seems to me now
As the remembrance of an idle gaud
Which in my childhood I did dote upon,
And all the faith, the virtue of my heart,
170 The object and the pleasure of mine eye,
Is only Helena. To her, my lord,
Was I betroth'd ere I saw Hermia.
But like a sickness did I loathe this food.
But, as in health, come to my natural taste,
175 Now I do wish it, long for it,
And will for evermore be true to it.

THESEUS

Fair lovers, you are fortunately met;
Of this **discourse** we more will hear anon.—
Egeus, I will overbear your will,
180 For in the temple, by and by, with us
These couples shall eternally be knit.—
And, for the morning now is something worn,
Our purpos'd hunting shall be set aside.

But, I think—for I want to be honest,
and now that I remember, this seems to be the case—   150
I came here with Hermia. It was our intention
to get away from Athens, to go somewhere where we might
escape Athenian law—

EGEUS

Enough! Enough, my lord! You have heard enough.
I beg you bring down the law upon his head.   155
They have run away—they would have, Demetrius!
They would have deprived you and me,
you of your wife and me of my consent—
my consent that she should be your wife.

DEMETRIUS

My lord, lovely Helen told me of their flight   160
and of their intention to come here to this woods.
And I, in a fury, followed them here,
with lovely Helena following me out of love.
But, my good lord, I don't know what power—
but some power has done it—my love for Hermia   165
has melted like the snow and now seems
like the memory of a worthless trinket
which I used to adore in my childhood.
Now all the faith and power of my heart
and the object and pleasure of my eyes   170
is Helena alone. I was engaged
to her before I saw Hermia.
But, like a sick person, I hated this food. (*Points to* HELENA.)
But now, like a healthy man, my natural taste has reformed.
Now, I want her, love her, long for her,   175
and I will always be true to her.

THESEUS

Beautiful lovers, you have happily reconciled.
I want to hear more about your story as soon as possible.
Egeus, I will overrule your wishes
because shortly, in the temple along with us,   180
these couples will be eternally joined in marriage.
Since the morning is somewhat spent,
our intended hunt will be postponed.

Away with us to Athens. Three and three,
185   We'll hold a feast in great solemnity.
Come, Hippolyta.

> [*Exeunt* THESEUS *and his* TRAIN, HIPPOLYTA, *and*
> EGEUS.]

DEMETRIUS
These things seem small and undistinguishable,
Like far-off mountains turned into clouds.

HERMIA
Methinks I see these things with parted eye,
190   When every thing seems double.

HELENA
                         So methinks;
And I have found Demetrius like a jewel,
Mine own, and not mine own.

DEMETRIUS
                      Are you sure
195   That we are awake? It seems to me
That yet we sleep, we dream. Do not you think
The Duke was here and bid us follow him?

HERMIA
Yea, and my father.

HELENA
               And Hippolyta.

LYSANDER
200   And he did bid us follow to the temple.

DEMETRIUS
Why, then, we are awake. Let's follow him,
And by the way let us **recount** our dreams.

> [*Exeunt* LOVERS.]

BOTTOM [*awaking*]
When my cue comes, call me, and I will answer. My next
is, "Most fair Pyramus." Heigh-ho! Peter Quince! Flute the
205   bellows-mender! Snout the tinker! Starveling! God's my
life! Stolen hence and left me asleep! I have had a most

Let's all go to Athens! Three men and three women—
we'll hold a wedding feast with great ceremony.   185
Come, Hippolyta.

    THESEUS, HIPPOLYTA, EGEUS, *and their* FOLLOWERS *all exit.*

DEMETRIUS
Everything seems small and undistinguishable,
like far-off mountains disappearing among clouds.

HERMIA
I think I see everything out of focus,
as when everything seems doubled.   190

HELENA
I think so, too.
And I have found Demetrius, like finding a jewel.
He is mine, and yet not mine.

DEMETRIUS
Are you sure
that we are awake? It seems to me   195
that we are still asleep, still dreaming. Don't you think
the Duke was here, and he told us to follow him?

HERMIA
Yes, and my father.

HELENA
And Hippolyta.

LYSANDER
And he told us to follow him to the temple.   200

DEMETRIUS
Well then, we are awake. Let's follow him,
and along the way, we'll tell each other our dreams.

    LOVERS *exit.*

BOTTOM (*awakening*)
When my cue comes, call me, and I will answer. My next line is,
"Most beautiful Pyramus." Hello! Peter Quince! Flute, the bellows-
mender! Snout, the tinker! Starveling! God bless me! They've   205
snuck away and left me asleep! I've had a most unusual dream.

rare vision. I have had a dream past the wit of man to say what dream it was. Man is but an ass if he go about to expound this dream. Methought I was—there is no man can tell what. Methought I was and methought I had—but man is but a patch'd fool* if he will offer to say what methought I had. The eye of man hath not heard, the ear of man hath not seen, man's hand is not able to taste, his tongue to conceive, nor his heart to report, what my dream was. I will get Peter Quince to write a ballad of this dream. It shall be called "Bottom's Dream" because it hath no bottom; and I will sing it in the latter end of a play, before the Duke. Peradventure, to make it the more gracious, I shall sing it at her death.

[*Exit.*]

---

211   *patch'd fool*   dressed like a professional fool, or jester

I've had a dream—it's beyond the power of human reason to
say what kind of dream it was. A man would be an ass if he
tried to explain this dream. I thought I was—there is no one who
can tell what. I thought I was—and I thought I had—but a   210
man would just be dressed like a fool if he would try to say
what I thought had happened. The eye of man has not heard, the
ear of man has not seen, man's hand isn't able to taste, his tongue
can't imagine, or his heart explain what my dream was about.
I will get Peter Quince to write a ballad about this dream.   215
It will be called "Bottom's Dream" because it doesn't have a
bottom. And I will sing it at the end of the play, before the
Duke. Perhaps to make it all the more gracious, I will sing it at
Thisbe's death.

BOTTOM *exits.*

ACT IV, SCENE II

[*Athens. Quince's house.*] *Enter* QUINCE, FLUTE, SNOUT, *and* STARVELING.

QUINCE
Have you sent to Bottom's house? Is he come home yet?

STARVELING
He cannot be heard of. Out of doubt he is transported.

FLUTE
If he come not, then the play is marr'd. It goes not forward, doth it?

QUINCE
5   It is not possible. You have not a man in all Athens able to discharge Pyramus but he.

FLUTE
No, he hath simply the best wit of any handicraftman in Athens.

SNOUT
Yea, and the best person too, and he is a very paramour
10   for a sweet voice.

FLUTE
You must say "**paragon**"; a "paramour" is, God bless us, a thing of naught.

Enter SNUG *the joiner.*

SNUG
Masters, the Duke is coming from the temple, and there is two or three lords and ladies more married. If our sport
15   had gone forward, we had all been made men.

FLUTE
O, sweet bully Bottom! Thus hath he lost a sixpence a day during his life. He could not have 'scaped sixpence a day. An the Duke had not given him sixpence a day for playing Pyramus, I'll be hang'd. He would have deserved it. Six
20   pence a day in Pyramus, or nothing.

ACT 4, SCENE 2

Athens. Quince's House. QUINCE, FLUTE, SNOUT, *and*
STARVELING *all enter.*

QUINCE

Have you sent someone to Bottom's house? Has he come home yet?

STARVELING

No one has heard a word about him. No doubt he has been
magically carried off.

FLUTE

If he doesn't come, then the play is ruined. The play won't go on,
will it?

QUINCE

It would be impossible. There's not a man in all Athens able to   5
portray Pyramus except him.

FLUTE

You're right. He simply has the best mind of any craftsman in
Athens.

SNOUT

Yes, and the best appearance, too. And he's a real paramour with
that sweet voice of his.   10

FLUTE

You mean "paragon." A "paramour" is—God bless us—a wicked
thing.

      SNUG *enters.*

SNUG

Gentlemen, the Duke is coming from the temple, and with him are
two or three more lords and ladies who have been married. If our
play had gone on, we'd all have made our fortunes.   15

FLUTE

Oh sweet, grand Bottom! He's lost a pension of sixpence a day for
life. He could not have escaped being given a sixpence a day. If
the Duke hadn't given him sixpence a day for playing Pyramus, I'll
be hanged! He would have deserved it. Either sixpence a day for
Pyramus or nothing!   20

Enter BOTTOM.

BOTTOM

Where are these lads? Where are these hearts?

QUINCE

Bottom! O most courageous day! O most happy hour!

BOTTOM

Masters, I am to discourse wonders. But ask me not what;
for, if I tell you, I am not true Athenian. I will tell you
25   everything right as it fell out.

QUINCE

Let us hear, sweet Bottom.

BOTTOM

Not a word of me. All that I will tell you is that the Duke
hath dined. Get your apparel together, good strings to
your beards,* new ribbons to your pumps. Meet presently
30   at the palace. Every man look o'er his part. For the short
and the long is, our play is preferr'd. In any case, let
Thisbe have clean linen, and let not him that plays the
lion pare his nails, for they shall hang out for the lion's
claws. And, most dear actors, eat no onions nor garlic, for
35   we are to utter sweet breath, and I do not doubt but to
hear them say it is a sweet comedy. No more words. Away!
Go, away!

     [*Exeunt.*]

28–29 *good . . . beards* strings to tie on false beards

BOTTOM *enters.*

BOTTOM

Where are my chums? Where are my hearties?

QUINCE

Bottom! Oh what a splendid day! Oh what a happy hour!

BOTTOM

Gentlemen, I have wonders to tell, but don't ask me what. If I tell you, I'm not a true Athenian. I will tell you everything, just as it came about.   25

QUINCE

Tell us, sweet Bottom.

BOTTOM

Not a word from me. All that I will tell you is that the Duke has eaten. Get your clothes together and good strings for your beards and new ribbons for your shoes. Meet me at the palace at once. Every one of you must review his part, for the long and short of it 30 is, our play has been recommended. Be sure that Thisbe has clean clothes, and don't let the one who plays the lion cut his nails because they should hang out like lion's claws. And, my dear actors, don't eat any onions or garlic, for we are to utter sweet 35 words, and I'm sure they'll say it's a sweet comedy. Not another word! Away! Go!

ALL *exit.*

Act IV Review

Discussion Questions

1. Reread Theseus's speech to the lovers in Scene i, lines 177–183. Why do you think he calls off the hunt?

2. Titania calls for music in Scene i. What are some of the ways music is used in this comedy?

3. Titania doesn't appear distressed to realize that she "gave" the boy back to Oberon when she was too in love with Bottom to care. Why do you think this doesn't seem to matter to her anymore?

4. In Scene i, Bottom says upon awakening, "Man is but an ass if he go about to expound this dream." What do you think are some possible meanings of that statement, both from Bottom's point of view and Shakespeare's?

5. For all of his blundering and pomposity, Bottom has some endearing qualities. What evidence of this do you see in this act?

6. Judging from the play so far, how do you think gender roles have changed since Shakespeare's time?

Literary Questions

1. **Hyperbole** means exaggeration used for effect. Find two examples of hyperbole in this scene and tell what you think they contribute.

2. In the second scene of Act IV, we return to the setting of Athens. What **contrasts** do you see as the setting shifts from forest to city?

3. Explain what you think the removal of the ass's head from Bottom **symbolizes** in the play. Can you find any other symbols in this act? Explain their possible meanings.

4. Shakespeare's language often employs figures of speech such as **similes**—comparisons of unlike things using *like* or *as*—and **metaphors**, which make the comparisons directly. Find some examples of similes and metaphors in this act, and explain what you think these comparisons contribute.

Writing Prompts

1. We never hear from the young boy who has been taken from his home to serve the fairy kingdom; he is only a pawn between Titania and Oberon. Write a journal entry that gives his account of events from his perspective as a grown man.

2. At the beginning of Scene i, the fairies surely notice that Bottom is wearing an ass's head. Yet at Titania's orders they wait upon him courteously. In Elizabethan language, write a scene with these characters on their own, complaining about the errands on which Bottom has sent them.

3. Misunderstandings are common in Shakespeare's comedies, and they are still a staple of this genre today. Consider romantic comedies you've seen in films or on television. Write about how misunderstandings are often crucial to their success.

4. Imagine you are a modern-day Oberon. Write a diary entry in which you struggle with whether the trick you played on Titania was fair. Discuss how you felt when you saw her doting on Bottom.

A Midsummer Night's Dream

ACT V

Open Air Theatre, 1994

*"The lunatic, the lover, and the poet
are of imagination all compact."*

Before You Read

1. Now that things are drawing to a conclusion, what tone do you expect the final act to take?

2. What loose ends need to be tied up in this act?

3. Dreams are often used as plot devices. Why do you think writers like them?

4. Watch for the ways in which the plot of the play about Pyramus and Thisbe parallels the plot of *A Midsummer Night's Dream*.

Literary Elements

1. **Imagery** is highly descriptive language that appeals to one or more of the five senses—taste, touch, hearing, smell, and sight. In Act I, Helena says about Hermia, "Your eyes are lodestars and your tongue's sweet air / More tuneable than lark to shepherd's ear / When wheat is green, when hawthorn buds appear." The variety of sensory images demonstrate what Demetrius finds attractive in Hermia.

2. The technique of **alliteration** repeats initial sounds—usually consonants—of words that are close together. For example, in Act I Hermia says of Demetrius, "he hath turn'd a heaven unto a hell!"

3. A **double entendre** is a statement that has two different meanings. In Act III, Scene ii, Demetrius says to Lysander, "I would I had your bond." He means "bond" in the sense of a binding legal agreement as well as the hold that Hermia holds over Lysander.

4. **Resolution** occurs when a conflict or confrontation is worked out. We have already seen the lovers pair off happily through the use of magic.

Words to Know

The following vocabulary words appear in Act V in the original text of Shakespeare's play. However, they are words that are still used today. Read the definitions here and pay attention to the words as you read the play (they will be in boldfaced type).

apt	suitable; likely
audacious	daring; bold
eloquence	powerful expressiveness
frenzy	wildness; intensity
habitation	home; place to live
palpable	able to be touched or felt
premeditated	prepared; thought of before
prodigious	strange; unusual
quell	stop; quiet
transfigured [transfigur'd]	changed; put into a new form

Act Summary

The company of actors earnestly performs their terrible play with the audience members—Theseus and Hippolyta especially—trying hard not to laugh. Oberon directs the fairies to scatter blessings upon Theseus's kingdom and especially upon the three couples who are to be married. After the wedding, the newly married lovers go off to bed.

The play concludes with a merry Puck telling the audience members that if they didn't like the play, they should pretend that they were dreaming during the time that they watched it.

Ian Richardson and Juliet Mills as Oberon and Titania, Royal Shakespeare Company, produced by Peter Hall

ACT V, SCENE I

[*Athens. The palace of Theseus.*] *Enter* THESEUS,
HIPPOLYTA, PHILOSTRATE, LORDS, *and*
ATTENDANTS.

HIPPOLYTA

'Tis strange, my Theseus, that these lovers speak of.

THESEUS

More strange than true. I never may believe
These antique fables, nor these fairy toys.
Lovers and madmen have such seething brains,
5   Such shaping fantasies, that apprehend
More than cool reason ever comprehends.
The lunatic, the lover, and the poet
Are of imagination all compact.
One sees more devils than vast hell can hold:
10   That is the madman. The lover, all as frantic,
See Helen's beauty in a brow of Egypt.*
The poet's eye, in a fine **frenzy** rolling,
Doth glance from heaven to earth, from earth to heaven,
And as imagination bodies forth
15   The forms of things unknown, the poet's pen
Turns them to shapes and gives to airy nothing
A local **habitation** and a name.
Such tricks hath strong imagination
That, if it would but apprehend some joy,
20   It comprehends some bringer of that joy;
Or in the night, imagining some fear,
How easy is a bush suppos'd a bear!

HIPPOLYTA

But all the story of the night told over,
And all their minds **transfigur'd** so together,
25   More witnesseth than fancy's images
And grows to something of great constancy,
But, howsoever, strange and admirable.

---

11   *Helen's . . . Egypt* Helen of Troy was a renowned Greek beauty. To the
Elizabethans, who valued a pale complexion, the dark face of a gypsy would be a
marked contrast to an ideal beauty.

ACT 5, SCENE 1

Athens. The palace of Theseus. THESEUS, HIPPOLYTA,
PHILOSTRATE, LORDS, *and* ATTENDANTS *all enter.*

HIPPOLYTA

These lovers speak of strange things, my Theseus.

THESEUS

It is more strange than true. I can never believe
these fanciful fables or these fairy fantasies.
Lovers and madmen have seething brains
and creative imaginations that conceive   5
more than cool reason ever comprehends.
The lunatic, the lover, and the poet
are entirely constructed out of imagination.
One of them sees more devils than far-reaching hell can hold—
that one is the madman. The lover, just as frantic,   10
sees beauty equal to Helen's in a gypsy's face.
The poet's eye, rolling in great frenzy,
glances from heaven to earth and from earth to heaven.
And as imagination calls into being
the forms of strange things, the poet's pen   15
forms them into shapes and gives these airy nothings
a home and a name.
A strong imagination is filled with such tricks
that if it wants to experience some joy,
it will dream of someone to bring that joy.   20
Or in the night, when one is imagining fearful things,
how easily imagination turns a bush into a bear!

HIPPOLYTA

But when the whole story of the night was told,
and all of their minds proved to be affected by the same delusion,
it emerges there is more to this than imagination's pictures,   25
and it becomes a story of great consistency.
At any rate, it is strange and wonderful.

Enter LOVERS: LYSANDER, DEMETRIUS, HERMIA,
and HELENA.

THESEUS
Here come the lovers, full of joy and mirth.—
Joy, gentle friends! Joy and fresh days of love
30   Accompany your hearts!

LYSANDER
               More than to us
Wait in your royal walks, your board, your bed!

THESEUS
Come now, what masques,* what dances shall we have
To wear away this long age of three hours
35   Between our after-supper and bedtime?
Where is our usual manager of mirth?
What revels are in hand? Is there no play
To ease the anguish of a torturing hour?
Call Philostrate.

PHILOSTRATE
40   Here, mighty Theseus.

THESEUS
Say, what abridgement have you for this evening?
What masque? What music? How shall we beguile
The lazy time, if not with some delight?

PHILOSTRATE
There is a brief how many sports are ripe.
45   Make choice of which your Highness will see first.

    [*giving* THESEUS *a paper*]

THESEUS [*Reads.*]
"The battle with the Centaurs,* to be sung
By an Athenian eunuch to the harp."
We'll none of that, that have I told my love

---

33 *masque* a form of entertainment consisting of dance and theatrics at which the
performers wore masks

46 *battle with the Centaurs* a well-known incident in the life of Hercules. The
Centaurs were supposedly half man, half horse.

The lovers LYSANDER, DEMETRIUS, HERMIA, *and* HELENA *all enter.*

THESEUS
Here come the lovers, full of joy and mirth.
Joy to you, gentle friends. May joy and the fresh days of love
stay in your hearts.   30

LYSANDER
May more joy than awaits us
wait for you in your royal walks, your table, and your bed!

THESEUS
Come, what masques and dances shall we have
to wear away the long three hours
between dessert and bedtime?   35
Where is our regular manager of entertainment?
What celebrations are on hand? Is there no play
to ease the anguish of a torturing hour?
Call Philostrate.

PHILOSTRATE
I am here, mighty Theseus.   40

THESEUS
Tell me, what pastime do you have for this evening?
What masque? What music? How shall we while away
the lazy time if not with some delightful entertainment?

PHILOSTRATE
Here is a list of the many delights that are ready.
Choose which one you will see first, your Highness.   45

He gives THESEUS *a paper.*

THESEUS (*Reads.*)
"The battle with the centaurs, to be sung
by an Athenian eunuch accompanied by a harp."
We'll have none of that. I have already told my love that story

In glory of my kinsman Hercules. [*Reads.*]
50   "The riot of the tipsy Bacchanals,
        Tearing the Thracian singer* in their rage."
        That is an old device; and it was play'd
        When I from Thebes came last a conqueror.
        "The thrice-three Muses* mourning for the death
55   Of learning, late deceas'd in beggary."
        That is some satire, keen and critical,
        Not sorting with a nuptial ceremony.
        "A tedious brief scene of young Pyramus
        And his love Thisbe, very tragical mirth."
60   "Merry" and "tragical"? "Tedious" and "brief"?
        That is hot ice and wondrous strange snow!
        How shall we find the concord of this discord?

PHILOSTRATE
        A play there is, my lord, some ten words long,
        Which is as brief as I have known a play;
65   But by ten words, my lord, it is too long,
        Which makes it tedious; for in all the play
        There is not one word **apt,** one player fitted.
        And tragical, my noble lord, it is.
        For Pyramus therein doth kill himself,
70   Which, when I saw rehears'd, I must confess,
        Made mine eyes water; but more merry tears
        The passion of loud laughter never shed.

THESEUS
        What are they that do play it?

PHILOSTRATE
        Hard-handed men that work in Athens here,
75   Which never labour'd in their minds till now,
        And now have toil'd their unbreath'd memories
        With this same play, against your nuptial.

THESEUS
        And we will hear it.

---

51   *Thracian singer* Orpheus, whose musical ability impressed men and gods alike.
      Orpheus was killed by frenzied, drunken devotees of the god of wine, Bacchus.

54   *Muses* Greek goddesses of the arts

to honor my kinsman Hercules. (*Reads.*)
"The riot of the tipsy Bacchanals   50
as they tear apart the singer Orpheus in their rage."
That is an old show, and it was played
when I last came from Thebes as a conqueror.
(*Reads.*) "The nine Muses mourning for the death
of Learning, who recently died a beggar."   55
That is a satire, sharp and critical.
It is not suited to a wedding ceremony.
(*Reads.*) "A tedious, brief scene about young Pyramus
and his lover Thisbe—a very tragic comedy."
"Merry" and "tragic"? "Tedious" and "brief"?   60
That is like hot ice and wonderfully strange snow.
How shall we find agreement between these contradictions?

PHILOSTRATE
It is a play, my lord, about ten words long,
which is as short a play as I have ever seen.
But even with just ten words, my lord, it is too long   65
and that's why it's tedious. For in all that play,
there is not one suitable word or one well-cast actor.
And it's tragic, my lord,
Pyramus does kill himself—
which, when I saw the play rehearsed, I must confess,   70
brought tears to my eyes. But merrier tears
were never shed.

THESEUS
Who are the people who perform this play?

PHILOSTRATE
They are laborers who work here in Athens,
but they never labored with their minds until now.   75
Now they are laboring with their unexercised memories
over this play, prepared for your wedding.

THESEUS
And we will see it.

PHILOSTRATE

No, my noble lord;
80 It is not for you. I have heard it over,
And it is nothing, nothing in the world,
Unless you can find sport in their intents,
Extremely stretch'd and conn'd with cruel pain,
To do you service.

THESEUS

I will hear that play;
85 For never anything can be amiss,
When simpleness and duty tender it.
Go, bring them in—and take your places, ladies.

[*Exit* PHILOSTRATE.]

HIPPOLYTA

I love not to see wretchedness o'er-charged,
90 And duty in his service perishing.

THESEUS

Why, gentle sweet, you shall see no such thing.

HIPPOLYTA

He says they can do nothing in this kind.

THESEUS

The kinder we, to give them thanks for nothing.
Our sport shall be to take what they mistake;
95 And what poor duty cannot do, noble respect
Takes it in might, not merit.
Where I have come, great clerks have purposed
To greet me with **premeditated** welcomes,
Where I have seen them shiver and look pale,
100 Make periods in the midst of sentences,
Throttle their practis'd accent in their fears,
And in conclusion dumbly have broke off,
Not paying me a welcome. Trust me, sweet,
Out of this silence yet I pick'd a welcome,
105 And in the modesty of fearful duty,
I read as much as from the rattling tongue
Of saucy and **audacious eloquence**.
Love, therefore, and tongue-ti'd simplicity
In least speak most, to my capacity.

PHILOSTRATE

No, my noble lord.
It is not for you. I have seen it,   80
and it is nothing—nothing in the world—
unless you can find amusement in their efforts,
which are extremely strained, and their lines which have been
memorized with great pain in order to serve you.

THESEUS

I will see their play,   85
for nothing can be wrong
when it is presented with simplicity and duty.
Go, bring them in. Take your places, ladies.

      PHILOSTRATE *exits.*

HIPPOLYTA

I don't like to see poor people pushed beyond their limits
in order to do you service.   90

THESEUS

Why, my gentle sweet, you shall see no such thing.

HIPPOLYTA

He says they cannot act at all.

THESEUS

Then we are all the kinder for thanking them for nothing.
Our amusement will be in accepting their blunders.
And whatever poor service they cannot do, our noble minds   95
will value the effort they make, not their ability.
On my travels, I have met great scholars who intended
to greet me with prepared welcoming speeches.
And I have seen them shiver and turn pale,
stop in the middle of sentences, and   100
choke on their rehearsed speeches in their fear.
In conclusion, they have silently broken off
without giving me a welcome. Trust me, sweet.
Out of their silence, I still picked out a welcome.
And in their shyness, caused by their respect for me,   105
I read as much as from a tongue wagging
with saucy and bold eloquence.
Therefore, love and tongue-tied modesty
speak the most when the least is said, as I see it.

Reenter PHILOSTRATE.

PHILOSTRATE

110   So please your Grace, the Prologue* is address'd.

THESEUS

Let him approach.

[*Flourish of trumpets.*]

Enter QUINCE *for the Prologue.*

QUINCE [*as* PROLOGUE]

If we, offend* it is with our goodwill.
    That you should think we come not to offend,
But with goodwill. To show our simple skill,

115   That is the true beginning of our end.
Consider, then, we come but in despite.
    We do not come, as minding to content you,
Our true intent is. All for your delight
    We are not here. That you should here repent you,

120   The actors are at hand, and, by their show
You shall know all that you are like to know.

[PROLOGUE *exits.*]

THESEUS

This fellow doth not stand upon points.*

LYSANDER

He hath rid his prologue like a rough colt; he knows not
the stop.* A good moral, my lord: it is not enough to

125   speak, but to speak true.

HIPPOLYTA

Indeed he hath play'd on this prologue like a child on a
recorder—a sound, but not in government.

---

110   *Prologue* introduces and explains a play. The player who gave these
introductions was known as the Prologue, too.

112   *If we, offend* . . . Quince pauses in the wrong places throughout his speech,
comically misreading his lines.

122   *stand upon points* a pun meaning both "careful about proper punctuation" and
"fastidious"

124   *stop* another pun, meaning both "to halt a horse" and "period"

PHILOSTRATE *enters.*

PHILOSTRATE

If it please your Grace, the Prologue is ready.   110

THESEUS

Let him approach.

> *There is a flourish of trumpets.*

> The PROLOGUE, QUINCE, *enters.*

QUINCE, *as* PROLOGUE

If we, offend you we do it with the best of intentions.
   You must believe that we have come not to offend,
But with good intentions. To show our simple skill,
   That is the real reason we are here.   115
Consider this then, that we come in spite of that.
   We did not come with the idea of pleasing you,
Our true intention is. For your pleasure,
   We are not here. So that you shall repent,
The actors are ready. And from their performance,   120
You will learn everything that you are likely to learn.

> PROLOGUE *exits.*

THESEUS

This fellow isn't one to worry about the finer points.

LYSANDER

He rode his prologue like a wild colt. He doesn't know what a stop
is. A good moral, my lord, is "It is not enough to speak, we must
speak correctly, too."   125

HIPPOLYTA

Indeed, he played on his prologue like a child plays on a
flute—a sound, but not under his control.

THESEUS

His speech was like a tangled chain—nothing impaired,
but all disordered. Who is next?

Enter with a trumpet before them, PYRAMUS
[(BOTTOM)] *and* THISBE [(FLUTE)], WALL
[(SNOUT)], MOONSHINE [(STARVELING)], LION
[(SNUG)], *and* PROLOGUE [(QUINCE)].

QUINCE [*as* PROLOGUE]

130   Gentles, perchance you wonder at this show;
        But wonder on till truth make all things plain.
      This man is Pyramus, if you would know;
        This beauteous lady Thisbe is certain.
      This man, with lime and roughcast, doth present
135   "Wall," that vile Wall which did these lovers sunder;
      And through Wall's chink, poor souls, they are content
        To whisper, at the which let no man wonder.
      This man, with lantern, dog, and bush of thorn,
        Presenteth "Moonshine," for, if you will know,
140   By moonshine did these lovers think no scorn
        To meet at Ninus's tomb, there, there to woo.
      This grisly beast, which "Lion" hight by name,
        The trusty Thisbe, coming first by night,
      Did scare away, or rather did affright;
145   And, as she fled, her mantle she did fall,
        Which Lion vile with bloody mouth did stain.
      Anon comes Pyramus, sweet youth and tall,
        And finds his trusty Thisbe's mantle slain;
      Whereat, with blade, with bloody blameful blade,
150   He bravely broach'd his boiling bloody breast;
      And Thisbe, tarrying in mulberry shade,
        His dagger drew, and died. For all the rest,
      Let Lion, Moonshine, Wall, and lovers twain
      At large discourse, while here thy do remain.

THESEUS

155   I wonder if the lion be to speak.

DEMETRIUS

No wonder, my lord; one lion may, when many asses do.

THESEUS

His speech was like a tangled chain. Nothing was broken, but it was all in disorder. Who is next?

> *A trumpet sounds.* PYRAMUS (BOTTOM), THISBE (FLUTE), WALL (SNOUT), MOONSHINE (STARVELING), *and* LION (SNUG), *and* PROLOGUE (QUINCE) *enter.*

QUINCE, *as* PROLOGUE

Ladies and gentlemen, perhaps you are wondering about this   130
display.
Well, wonder on until truth makes everything clear.
This man is Pyramus, if you want to know.
This beautiful lady is Thisbe, indeed.
This man, covered with soil and plaster, represents
The wall—that horrible wall which separated these lovers.   135
And through a crack in the wall, poor souls, they are content
To whisper. None of you must be amazed by this.
This man with the lantern, dog, and thornbush
Represents Moonshine. Because, if you would like to know,
These lovers are not ashamed to meet   140
By moonlight at Ninus's tomb to kiss and court.
This terrible beast which is called a lion,
Scares away the trusting Thisbe, who comes first that night,
Or rather, frightens her.
And as she runs away, she drops her cloak   145
Which the lion stains with his horrible bloody mouth.
Soon along comes Pyramus, a sweet, brave young man,
And finds his trusting Thisbe's cloak destroyed.
When he sees this, with his sword—his bloody, deadly sword—
He bravely stabs his boiling, bloody breast.   150
Then Thisbe, hiding in the dark shadows,
Drew his dagger and killed herself. As for all the rest,
Let Lion, Moonshine, Wall, and lovers together,
Tell you at length while they are here.

THESEUS

I wonder if the lion will speak.   155

DEMETRIUS

It would not be a surprise, my lord. One lion might when so many asses do.

[*Exeunt* LION, THISBE, MOONSHINE *and*
PROLOGUE.]

SNOUT [*as* WALL]
In this same interlude it doth befall
That I, one Snout by name, present a wall;
And such a wall, as I would have you think,
160   That had in it a crannied hole or chink,
Through which the lovers, Pyramus and Thisbe,
Did whisper often very secretly.
This loam, this roughcast, and this stone doth show
That I am that same wall. The truth is so.
165   And this the cranny is, right and sinister,
Through which the fearful lovers are to whisper.

THESEUS
Would you desire lime and hair to speak better?

DEMETRIUS
It is the wittiest partition that ever I heard discourse,
    my lord.

THESEUS
170   Pyramus draws near the wall. Silence!

BOTTOM [*as* PYRAMUS]
O grim-look'd night! O night with hue black!
    O night, which ever art when day is not!
O night, O night! Alack, alack, alack,
    I fear my Thisbe's promise is forgot!
175   And thou, O wall, O sweet, O lovely wall,
    That stand'st between her father's ground and mine!
Thou wall, O wall, O sweet and lovely wall,
    Show me thy chink, to blink through with mine eyne!

    [WALL *holds up his fingers.*]

Thanks, courteous wall; Jove shield thee well for this!
180   But what see I? No Thisbe do I see.
O wicked wall, through whom I see no bliss,
    Curs'd be thy stones for thus deceiving me!

PROLOGUE, THISBE, LION, *and* MOONSHINE *exit.*

SNOUT, *as* WALL
During this part, it happens
that I, Snout by name, represent a wall.
And it is such a wall, as I would have you know,
that has a hole or crack in it   160
through which the lovers Pyramus and Thisbe
often whispered, very secretly.
This soil, this plaster, and this stone show
that I am that very wall. It is the truth.
And this is the crack, which runs horizontally *(shows crack,*   165
   with his fingers),
through which the frightened lovers will whisper.

THESEUS
Could you want plaster and hair to speak any better?

DEMETRIUS
It is the most intelligent wall I ever heard speak, my lord.

THESEUS
Pyramus is nearing the wall. Silence!   170

BOTTOM, *as* PYRAMUS
Oh grim night! Oh night with such a black color!
   Oh night, which is always here when day is not!
Oh night, Oh night! Alas, alas, alas,
   I am afraid my Thisbe has forgotten her promise.
And you, Oh wall, Oh sweet, Oh lovely wall,   175
   You stand between her father's property and mine!
You wall, Oh wall, Oh sweet and lovely wall,
   Show me your crack, so I can peer through it with my eyes.

      THE WALL *holds up his fingers.*

Thanks, courteous wall. May God protect you well for this!
   But what do I see? I do not see Thisbe.   180
Oh wicked wall, through whom I see no happiness,
   May your stones be cursed for deceiving me like this!

Act 5, Scene 1   195

THESEUS

The wall, methinks, being sensible, should curse again.

BOTTOM

No, in truth, sir, he should not. "Deceiving me" is Thisbe's
185　　cue. She is to enter now, and I am to spy her through the
wall. You shall see it will fall pat as I told you. Yonder she
comes.

　　　　　Enter THISBE [FLUTE].

FLUTE　[*as* THISBE]

O wall, full often hast thou heard my moans
　　For parting my fair Pyramus and me.
190　My cherry lips have often kiss'd thy stones,
　　Thy stones with lime and hair knit up in thee.

BOTTOM　[*as* PYRAMUS]

I see a voice! Now will I to the chink,
　　To spy an I can hear my Thisbe's face.*
Thisbe?

FLUTE　[*as* THISBE]

195　　　　　My love, thou art my love, I think.

BOTTOM　[*as* PYRAMUS]

　　Think what thou wilt, I am thy lover's grace;
And, like Limander,* am I trusty still.

FLUTE　[*as* THISBE]

And I like Helen, till the Fates me kill.

BOTTOM　[*as* PYRAMUS]

Not Shafalus to Procrus* was so true.

FLUTE　[*as* THISBE]

200　As Shafalus to Procrus, I to you.

BOTTOM　[*as* PYRAMUS]

O, kiss me through the hole of this vile wall!

192-93　*see . . . face* Bottom is confusing his lines.

　197　*Limander* Bottom means Leander. Leander swam the Hellespont every night to
　　　see Hero—not Helen as Flute declares in the next line.

　199　*Shafalus . . . Procrus* Another of Bottom's humorous mistakes. He really means
　　　Cephalus, who was married to Procrus. Cephalus resisted Aurora and
　　　remained true to Procus.

THESEUS

I think the wall, having feelings, should curse in return.

BOTTOM

No, in truth, sir, he should not. "Deceiving me" is Thisbe's cue.
She will enter now, and I will see her through the wall. You will 185
see it happen exactly the way I told you. There she comes.

THISBE (*as* FLUTE) *enters.*

FLUTE, *as* THISBE

Oh wall, so often you have heard my moans
   Because you separate my beautiful Pyramus and me!
My cherry lips have often kissed your stones— 190
   Your stones made up of plaster and of hair.

BOTTOM, *as* PYRAMUS

I see a voice! Now I will go to the crack
   to see if I can hear my Thisbe's face.
Thisbe!

FLUTE, *as* THISBE

My love! You are my love, I think. 195

BOTTOM, *as* PYRAMUS

   Think what you will, I am your gracious lover.
And, like Limander, I am still faithful.

FLUTE, *as* THISBE

And I will be as faithful as Helen until the Fates kill me.

BOTTOM, *as* PYRAMUS

Not even Shafalus was as faithful to Procus.

FLUTE, *as* THISBE

As true as Shafalus was to Procus, I am to you. 200

BOTTOM, *as* PYRAMUS

Oh kiss me through the hole of this horrid wall!

FLUTE [*as* THISBE]

I kiss the wall's hole, not your lips at all.

BOTTOM [*as* PYRAMUS]

Wilt thou at Ninny's tomb meet me straightway?

FLUTE [*as* THISBE]

'Tide life, 'tide death, I come without delay.

[*Exeunt* BOTTOM *and* FLUTE.]

SNOUT [*as* WALL]

205   Thus have I, Wall, my part discharged so;
And, being done, thus Wall away doth go.

[*Exit.*]

THESEUS

Now is the moon used between the two neighbours.

DEMETRIUS

No remedy, my lord, when walls are so willful to hear
without warning.

HIPPOLYTA

210   This is the silliest stuff that ever I heard.

THESEUS

The best in this kind are but shadows; and the worst are
no worse, if imagination amend them.

HIPPOLYTA

It must be your imagination, then, and not theirs.

THESEUS

If we imagine no worse of them than they of themselves,
215   they may pass for excellent men. Here come two noble
beasts in, a man and a lion.

Enter LION [(SNUG)] *and* MOONSHINE
[(STARVELING)].

FLUTE, *as* THISBE

I can only kiss the wall's hole, not your lips at all.

BOTTOM, *as* PYRAMUS

Will you meet me right away at Ninny's tomb?

FLUTE, *as* THISBE

Let life or death come, I will meet you without delay.

    BOTTOM and FLUTE exit.

SNOUT, *as* WALL

Now I, Wall, have finished performing my part.   205
And since I am done, Wall will go away.

    He exits.

THESEUS

Now the wall is down between the two neighbors.

DEMETRIUS

This doesn't help the situation, my lord, when walls are so ready to listen without warning others of mischief.

HIPPOLYTA

This is the silliest stuff I have ever heard.   210

THESEUS

Even the best plays are merely shadows. And the worst are no worse if imagination comes to their aid.

HIPPOLYTA

Then it must be the imagination you supply, and not theirs.

THESEUS

If we imagine no worse of them than they think of themselves, they may pass for excellent men. Here come two noble   215
beasts, a man and a lion.

    LION (SNUG) and MOONSHINE (STARVELING) enter.

SNUG [*as* LION]
You, ladies, you, whose gentle hearts do fear
 The smallest monstrous mouse that creeps on floor,
May now perchance both quake and tremble here,
220   When lion rough in wildest rage doth roar.
Then know that I, as Snug the joiner, am
A lion fell, nor else no lion's dam;
For, if I should as lion come in strife
Into this place, 'twere pity on my life.

THESEUS
225 A very gentle beast, and of a good conscience.

DEMETRIUS
The very best at a beast, my lord, that e'er I saw.

LYSANDER
This lion is a very fox for his valour.

THESEUS
True, and a goose for his discretion.

DEMETRIUS
Not so, my lord, for his valour cannot carry his discretion,
230 and the fox carries the goose.

THESEUS
His discretion, I am sure, cannot carry his valour, for the
goose carries not the fox. It is well. Leave it to his
discretion, and let us hearken to the moon.

STARVELING [*as* MOONSHINE]
This lantern doth the horned moon present;—

DEMETRIUS
235 He should have worn the horns on his head.*

THESEUS
He is no crescent, and his horns are invisible within the
circumference.

STARVELING [*as* MOONSHINE]
This lantern doth the horned moon present.
 Myself the man i' th' moon do seem to be.

---

235 *horns on his head* a joke about a cuckold (a man whose wife is cheating on him)
who has horns

SNUG, *as* LION
You ladies, you whose gentle hearts fear
　The smallest monstrous mouse that crawls on the floor,
May now perhaps shake and tremble here
　When a rough lion roars in wildest rage. 　　　　220
So you must know that I am Snug the joiner—
Only the skin of a lion—not even a lioness.
For, if I should come as an angry lion
Into this place, it would mean my head.

THESEUS
He's a very polite beast and has a good conscience. 　　225

DEMETRIUS
He is the very best beast, my lord, that I have ever seen.

LYSANDER
This lion is more foxy than he is brave.

THESEUS
True, and he is a goose in his discretion.

DEMETRIUS
No, my lord, because his bravery will never carry away his
discretion and the fox carries away the goose. 　　230

THESEUS
I am sure his discretion cannot take away his courage because
the goose does not carry away the fox. That is as it should be.
Leave it to his discretion, and let us listen to the moon.

STARVELING, *as* MOONSHINE
This lantern represents the horned moon—

DEMETRIUS
He should have worn the horns on his own head. 　　235

THESEUS
He is not a crescent moon. His horns are invisible within the
circle of the full moon.

STARVELING, *as* MOONSHINE
This lantern represents the horned moon.
　I am supposed to be the man in the moon.

THESEUS

240   This is the greatest error of all the rest. The man should be put into the lantern. How is it else "the man i' th' moon"?

DEMETRIUS

He dares not come there for the candle; for, you see, it is already in snuff.*

HIPPOLYTA

I am aweary of this moon. Would he would change!

THESEUS

245   It appears, by his small light of discretion, that he is in the wane; but yet, in courtesy, in all reason, we must stay the time.

LYSANDER

Proceed, Moon.

STARVELING [*as* MOONSHINE]

All that I have to say, is to tell you that the lanthorn is the
250   moon, I the man i' th' moon, this thorn-bush my thorn-bush; and this dog my dog.

DEMETRIUS

Why, all these should be in the lantern, for all these are in the moon. But silence. Here comes Thisbe.

      Reenter THISBE [(FLUTE)].

FLUTE [*as* THISBE]

This is old Ninny's tomb. Where is my love?

SNUG [*as* LION]

255   [*roaring*] O—

      [*The* LION *roars.* THISBE *runs off, dropping her mantle.*]

DEMETRIUS

Well roar'd, Lion.

THESEUS

Well run, Thisbe.

---

243   *in snuff* means both "offended" and "in need of snuffing"

THESEUS

This is a greater mistake than all the rest. The man should be   240
inside the lantern. How else can he be the man in the moon?

DEMETRIUS

He does not dare go there on account of the candle, because,
you see, it already needs snuffing.

HIPPOLYTA

I am tired of this moon. I wish he would change!

THESEUS

It appears, judging by his dim intelligence, that he is waning.   245
Yet, out of courtesy and in all reason, we must wait him out.

LYSANDER

Go on, Moon.

STARVELING, *as* MOONSHINE

All I have to say is to tell you that the lantern is the moon. I am
the man in the moon. This thornbush is my thornbush, and   250
this dog is my dog.

DEMETRIUS

Why, all of these should be in the lantern, because all of these are
in the moon. But silence! Here comes Thisbe.

> FLUTE, *as* THISBE, *reenters.*

FLUTE, *as* THISBE

This is old Ninny's tomb. Where is my love?

SNUG, *as* LION

Oh!   255

> The LION *roars and* THISBE *runs off, dropping her coat.*

DEMETRIUS

Well-roared, Lion!

THESEUS

Well-run, Thisbe!

HIPPOLYTA

Well shone, Moon. Truly, the moon shines with a
good grace.

[*The* LION *shakes* THISBE'S *mantle and exits.*]

THESEUS

260 Well mous'd, Lion.

Reenter PYRAMUS [(BOTTOM)].

DEMETRIUS

And then came Pyramus.

[LION *exits.*]

LYSANDER

And so the lion vanish'd.

BOTTOM [*as* PYRAMUS]

Sweet Moon, I thank thee for thy sunny beams.
 I thank thee, Moon, for shining now so bright;

265 For, by thy gracious, golden, glittering gleams,
 I trust to take of truest Thisbe sight.—
  But stay, O spite!
  But mark, poor knight,
 What dreadful dole is here!

270 Eyes, do you see?
  How can it be?
 O dainty duck! O dear!
  Thy mantle good,
  What, stain'd with blood!

275 Approach, ye Furies* fell!
  O Fates, come, come,
  Cut thread and thrum;
 Quail, crush, conclude, and **quell**!

THESEUS

This passion, and the death of a dear friend, would go
280 near to make a man look sad.

HIPPOLYTA

Beshrew my heart but I pity the man.

---

275 *Furies* three deities who pursued and punished human wrongdoers

HIPPOLYTA

Well-shone, Moon! Truly, the moon shines very graciously.

The LION *shakes* THISBE'S *cloak and exits.*

THESEUS

Well-shaken, Lion!   260

PYRAMUS (BOTTOM) *reenters.*

DEMETRIUS

And now comes Pyramus.

LION *exits.*

LYSANDER

And the Lion has disappeared.

BOTTOM, *as* PYRAMUS

Sweet Moon, I thank you for your sunny beams.
    I thank you, Moon, for shining so bright.
For, by your gracious, golden, glittering gleams,   265
    I hope to catch sight of my loyal Thisbe.
        But wait! Oh trouble!
        But what is this, poor knight?
    What sorrowful thing is this?
        Eyes, do you see?   270
        How can it be?
    Oh dainty duck! Oh dear!
        Your good cloak.
        Is this, stained with blood?
    Come here, you dreadful Furies!   275
        Come, come, you Fates!
        End it all
    Overpower, crush, end, and kill!

THESEUS

All this grief and the death of a dear friend would almost
make a man look sad.   280

HIPPOLYTA

Curse my heart, but I pity the man.

BOTTOM [*as* PYRAMUS]
O wherefore Nature, didst thou lions frame?
　　Since lion vile hath here deflow'r'd my dear;
Which is—no, no—which was the fairest dame
285　That liv'd, that lov'd, that lik'd, that look'd with cheer.
　　　　"Come, tears, confound;
　　　　Out, sword, and wound
　　The pap of Pyramus;
　　　　Ay, that left pap,
290　　　Where heart doth hop."

　　[*Stabs himself.*]

"Thus die I, thus, thus, thus.
　　　　Now am I dead;
　　　　Now am I fled;
　　My soul is in the sky.
295　　　Tongue, lose thy light;
　　　　Moon, take thy flight."

　　[*Exit* MOONSHINE.]

Now die, die, die, die, die.

　　[PYRAMUS *dies.*]

DEMETRIUS
No die, but an ace, for him, for he is but one.

LYSANDER
Less than an ace, man, for he is dead, he is nothing.

THESEUS
300　With the help of a surgeon he might yet recover and yet
prove an ass.

HIPPOLYTA
How chance Moonshine is gone before Thisbe comes back
and finds her lover?

THESEUS
She will find him by starlight.

　　Reenter THISBE [(FLUTE)].

305　Here she comes, and her passion ends the play.

BOTTOM, *as* PYRAMUS
Why, O Nature, did you create lions?
    A vile lion has here destroyed my love.
She is—no!—she was the loveliest girl
    Who ever lived, who loved, who liked, who looked with a face. 285
        Come, tears, kill me!
        Out, sword, and wound
    The breast of Pyramus.
        Yes, the left breast
        Where the heart beats. 290

    (Stabs himself.)

So I die—thus, thus, thus.
    Now I am dead.
    Now I am gone.
My soul is in the sky.
    Tongue, lose your speech. 295
    Moon, fly away.

    (MOONSHINE *exits.*)

Now—die, die, die, die, die.

    (PYRAMUS *dies.*)

DEMETRIUS
Not even a single die for him, but an ace, for he is just one.

LYSANDER
He's less than an ace, man, because he's dead; he's nothing.

THESEUS
With the help of a surgeon, he might still recover, and prove 300
himself an ass still.

HIPPOLYTA
How can it be that Moonshine is gone before Thisbe comes back
and finds her lover?

THESEUS
She will find him by starlight.

        FLUTE, *as* THISBE, *enters.*

Here she comes. Her passionate speech ends the play. 305

HIPPOLYTA

Methinks she should not use a long one for such a
Pyramus. I hope she will be brief.

DEMETRIUS

A mote will turn the balance, which Pyramus, which
Thisbe, is the better: he for a man, God warrant us; she for
a woman, God bless us.

LYSANDER

She hath spied him already with those sweet eyes.

DEMETRIUS

And thus she means, *videlicet*—

FLUTE [*as* THISBE]

"Asleep, my love?
   What, dead, my dove?
O Pyramus, arise!
   Speak, speak! Quite dumb?
   Dead, dead? A tomb
Must cover thy sweet eyes.
   These lily lips,*
   This cherry nose,
These yellow cowslip cheeks,
   Are gone, are gone!
   Lovers, make moan.
His eyes were green as leeks.*
   O Sisters Three,*
   Come, come to me,
With hands as pale as milk.
   Lay them in gore,
   Since you have shore
With shears his thread of silk.
   Tongue, not a word!
   Come, trusty sword;
Come, blade, my breast imbrue!

[*Stabs herself.*]

---

319 *lily lips . . .* Flute makes a humorous jumble of his speech. "Cherry lips,"
    "yellow cowslip hair," etc., would be more appropriate.

324 *leeks* green onions

325 *Sisters Three* the Furies

HIPPOLYTA
I think she should not make a long speech for such a
Pyramus as this. I hope she will be brief.

DEMETRIUS
A speck of dust would tip the scales whether Pyramus or
Thisbe is better. He as a man, God save us! Or she as
a woman, God bless us!   310

LYSANDER
She has already spied him with those sweet eyes.

DEMETRIUS
And so she complains, as follows:

FLUTE, *as* THISBE
    Asleep, my love?
    What? Dead, my dove?
Oh Pyramus, arise!   315
    Speak, speak! Completely mute?
    Dead, dear? A tomb
Must cover your sweet eyes.
    These lily lips,
    This cherry nose,   320
These yellow cowslip cheeks,
    Are gone, are gone!
    Lovers, you must moan.
His eyes were as green as leeks.
    Oh you three sisters of Fate.   325
    Come, come to me,
With hands as white as milk.
    Dip them in blood,
    Since you have cut
With shears his thread of silk.   330
    Tongue, don't say a word!
    Come, trusty sword;
Come, blade, stain my breast with blood.

    (FLUTE, *as* THISBE, *stabs herself.*)

And, farewell, friends;
335   Thus, Thisbe ends.
    Adieu, adieu, adieu."

        [*Dies.*]

THESEUS
    Moonshine and Lion are left to bury the dead.

DEMETRIUS
    Ay, and Wall too.

BOTTOM [*starting up*]
    No, I assure you, the wall is down that parted their
340   fathers. Will it please you to see the Epilogue, or to hear
    a Bergomask dance* between two of our company?

THESEUS
    No epilogue, I pray you, for your play needs no excuse.
    Never excuse. For when the players are all dead, there
    need none to be blamed. Marry, if he that writ it had
345   played Pyramus and hang'd himself in Thisbe's garter, it
    would have been a fine tragedy; and so it is, truly; and
    very notably discharg'd. But, come, your Bergomask; let
    your epilogue alone.

        [*A dance.*]

    The iron tongue of midnight hath told twelve.
350   Lovers, to bed; 'tis almost fairy time.
    I fear we shall out-sleep the coming morn
    As much as we this night have overwatch'd.
    This **palpable**-gross play hath well beguil'd
    The heavy gait of night. Sweet friends, to bed.
355   A fortnight hold we this solemnity
    In nightly revels and new jollity.

        [*Exeunt.*]

        Enter ROBIN GOODFELLOW.

ROBIN GOODFELLOW
    Now the hungry lion roars,
        And the wolf behowls the moon;

---

341   *Bergomask dance* a rustic dance named for the country people of Bergamo, Italy

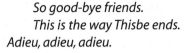

> *So good-bye friends.*
> *This is the way Thisbe ends.*   335
> *Adieu, adieu, adieu.*

> *(She dies.)*

THESEUS

Moonshine and Lion are left to bury the dead.

DEMETRIUS

Yes, and Wall, too.

BOTTOM (*starting to get up*)

No, I assure you, the wall that separated their fathers is down.
Would you like to see the Epilogue or hear a dance by two   340
men of our company?

THESEUS

No epilogue, I beg you, for your play needs no explanations.
Never explain because when the actors are all dead, there is no
one to be blamed. Indeed, if the author had played Pyramus and
hanged himself by Thisbe's garter, it would have been a fine   345
tragedy. And so it is, truly, and very remarkably presented. But,
come, your dance. Forget your epilogue.

> *The actors dance and then exit.*

The iron bell has struck twelve.
Lovers, go to bed; it is almost fairy time.   350
I am afraid we will outsleep the coming morning,
since we have stayed up so late tonight.
This obviously crude play has cheated
the sleepy pace of night. Sweet friends, go to bed.
For two weeks we'll hold this celebration   355
in nightly entertainments and new delights.

> *They exit.*

> PUCK *enters with a broom.*

PUCK

> Now the hungry lion roars,
>   and the wolf howls at the moon,

Whilst the heavy ploughman snores,
360   All with weary task fordone.
Now the wasted brands do glow,
    Whilst the screech-owl, screeching loud,
Puts the wretch that lies in woe
    In remembrance of a shroud.
365 Now it is the time of night
    That the graves, all gaping wide,
Every one lets forth his sprite,
    In the church-way paths to glide.
And we fairies, that do run
370   By the triple Hecate's* team
From the presence of the sun,
    Following darkness like a dream,
Now are frolic. Not a mouse
Shall disturb this hallowed house.
375 I am sent with broom before,
To sweep the dust behind the door.

    Enter OBERON *and* TITANIA *with their* TRAIN.

OBERON

Through the house give glimmering light,
    By the dead and drowsy fire,
Every elf and fairy sprite,
380   Hop as light as bird from brier;
And this ditty, after me,
Sing, and dance it trippingly.

TITANIA

First, rehearse your song by rote,
To each word a warbling note.
385 Hand in hand, with fairy grace,
Will we sing, and bless this place.

    [*Song and dance.*]

OBERON

Now, until the break of day,
Through this house each fairy stray.
To the best bride-bed will we,

---

370   *Hecate* "triple" because she was known by three names. She was a goddess of the
moon (and, therefore, abroad at night like the fairies).

While the sleeping plowman snores,
  Exhausted from his weary tasks.   360
Now the used-up firewood glows,
  While the screech owl, screeching loud,
Makes the wretched man who lies in pain
  Think of a coffin.
Now is the time of night   365
  That graves, all wide open,
Each lets forth a ghost
  To glide down the church paths.
And we fairies—who run
  Beside the three-named Hecate's team   370
From the presence of the sun,
  Following darkness like a dream—
Now we are merry. Not a mouse
Shall disturb this sacred house.
I have been sent ahead with a broom   375
To sweep the dust from behind the door.

  OBERON *and* TITANIA *enter with all their* FOLLOWERS.

OBERON
Through this house, give glimmering light
  From the dead and sleepy fire.
Every elf and fairy,
  Hop as lightly as a bird from a twig.   380
And sing this song after me,
And dance it with spirit.

TITANIA
First, rehearse your song from memory.
To each word, add a musical note.
Hand in hand, with fairy grace,   385
We will sing and bless this place.

  Song and dance.

OBERON
Now, until the break of day,
Each fairy must scatter through this house.
We will go to the best bridal bed,

390   Which by us shall blessed be;
      And the issue there create
      Ever shall be fortunate.
      So shall all the couples three
      Ever true in loving be,
395   And the blots of Nature's hand
      Shall not in their issue stand.
      Never mole, harelip, nor scar,
      Nor mark **prodigious**, such as are
      Despised in nativity,
400   Shall upon their children be.
      With this field-dew consecrate,
      Every fairy take his gait,
      And each several chamber bless,
      Through this palace, with sweet peace;
405   And the owner of it blest
      Ever shall in safety rest.
      Trip away; make no stay;
      Meet me all by break of day.

      [*Exeunt* OBERON, TITANIA, *and* TRAIN.]

ROBIN GOODFELLOW
      If we shadows have offended,
410   Think but this, and all is mended:
      That you have but slumber'd here
      While these visions did appear.
      And this weak and idle theme,
      No more yielding but a dream,
415   Gentles, do not reprehend.
      If you pardon, we will mend.
      And, as I am an honest Puck,
      If we have unearned luck
      Now to 'scape the serpent's tongue,
420   We will make amends ere long.
      Else the Puck a liar call.
      So, good night unto you all.
      Give me your hands, if we be friends,
      And Robin shall restore amends.

      [*Exit.*]

Which will be blessed by us. 390
And the children there conceived
Shall always be fortunate.
Also, all three couples shall
Be forever lovingly faithful.
And Nature's occasional deformities 395
Shall not appear in their children.
Not a mole, harelip, or scar,
Or unnatural birthmark, such as are
Despised in newborn babies,
Will be upon their children. 400
With this consecrated dew from the field,
Every fairy make his way
And bless each and every chamber
Throughout this palace with sweet peace.
And the owner of it, once blessed, 405
Will rest forever in safety.
Skip away; do not stop.
All of you meet me at break of day.

All exit except PUCK.

PUCK

If we shadows have offended you
Just imagine this and all will be mended: 410
Imagine that you were just sleeping here
While these visions appeared.
And this weak and silly play
Is no more than a dream.
Gentlemen and ladies do not scold us. 415
If you forgive us, we'll make amends.
And, as I am honest Puck,
If we have the undeserved luck
To escape the hissing of the audience,
We'll make it up to you before long. 420
If we do not, call Puck a liar.
So, good night to you all.
Give me your applause, if we are friends.
And Robin will make amends.

PUCK *exits.*

Act V Review

Discussion Questions

1. These lines of Theseus from Act V are well known: ". . . in the night, imagining some fear, / How easy is a bush suppos'd a bear." Describe a time when you or someone you know allowed fear to carry the imagination away.

2. How would you sum up the Athenians' attitude toward the play-within-the-play?

3. During the play, Theseus tells Hippolyta that until an audience uses its imagination, even the best plays are only shadows. Explain whether or not you think that is true.

4. Early in the play, Oberon seems to resent Theseus because Oberon's wife, Titania, once loved him. Now he is full of goodwill. What do you think accounts for his change of heart?

5. Much of this play doesn't rhyme, but some parts do. Compare and contrast the tone, intention, and effect of the poems spoken by Snout as The Wall (lines 157-166) and by Robin Goodfellow, also known as Puck (lines 409-424).

Literary Elements

1. *A Midsummer Night's Dream* is filled with **imagery**—word pictures that appeal to the five senses and add emotion and power to the writing. Find examples of sensory images in Act V, and explain what they contribute to the play.

2. **Alliteration** refers to the repetition of initial sounds in words that that are close together. Find an example of alliteration in Act V. What do you think the use of this technique adds to the play?

3. A phrase that can be interpreted in more than one way is a **double entendre**. When Theseus wonders aloud if the lion is about to speak, Demetrius answers " . . . one lion may, when many asses do." What makes this a double entendre?

4. By the end of the play, the Athenians from the city and the fairies and lovers in the woods have been brought together and **resolution** is achieved. What are some issues and conflicts that get resolved?

Writing Prompts

1. Reread Theseus's speech (lines 2–22) in which he compares the lunatic, the poet, and the lover, and implies that all three are to be pitied. Using a chart, list what you think are the characteristics of each. Make a fourth list of characteristics that are shared among the three. Now write a short essay explaining why you do or don't agree with Theseus, and whether or not you think Shakespeare himself would.

2. Reread the dialogue between Theseus and Hippolyta in lines 85–109. In a short essay, discuss what it reveals about each of them, their relationship, and their prospects for a good marriage.

3. Write a review of the play-within-the-play. Use a satirical tone if you like.

4. Imagine that you are either Helena or Demetrius. In the language of Shakespeare's era, write your own vows for the wedding.

The Play in Review

Discussion and Analysis

1. *A Midsummer Night's Dream* is considered the most popular of Shakespeare's comedies. What do you think accounts for its popularity?

2. Fairies and magic are important aspects of this play. Say whether you think they are used effectively, and discuss some other ways they could have been used.

3. Some critics say that in *A Midsummer Night's Dream*, the ideas are more important than the characters. Explain why you do or don't agree.

4. One message of this comedy is that as much as we pride ourselves on being rational, some important aspects of our lives are irrational and beyond our control. Other than romantic love, what other aspects of our lives are sometimes beyond our control?

5. Which do you think is worse, not being able to capture the heart of the person you think you love, or developing a relationship with that person and discovering they are not who you thought they were? Explain.

6. In Act III, Scene ii, Helena says, "Sleep, that sometimes shuts up sorrow's eye, / Steal me awhile from mine own company." Discuss a time when you or someone you know tried to escape a difficult situation by sleeping. Did sleep help?

7. Film critic Roger Ebert has posed the question of why so many Shakespeare plays continue to be filmed despite the absence of car chases and explosions. How would you answer?

Literary Elements

1. Shakespeare wrote most of *A Midsummer Night's Dream* in **iambic pentameter**—lines which typically have ten syllables, with every other syllable stressed or accented. Scan some lines from the play and see if you can find this pattern. Also look for other verse forms in the play, such as the song the fairies sing to Titania in Act II, Scene ii. What do you think are some reasons that Shakespeare uses different forms in the same play?

2. Even Shakespeare's comedies are rich in **themes**—the main ideas, or messages, that the writer wants to convey in a work of literature. With your classmates, discuss some of the themes found in *A Midsummer Night's Dream*.

3. An **allusion** is a reference to a historical or literary figure, happening, or event that is meant to enhance the story. In this play, one of the allusions is to Cupid, the Greek god of love. Find another allusion and explain its meaning and how it adds to the play.

4. The rich **diction**, or word choice, in *A Midsummer Night's Dream* has provided English with some well-known phrases. Search for as many lines or phrases from the play as you can that sound familiar to you.

5. Who do you think is the most memorable **character** in this play? Support your answer with examples from the text.

6. A **paradox** is someone or something with apparently contradictory qualities. It is paradoxical that Helena—like Demetrius's dog—grows fonder of him the more he mistreats her. Find some other examples of paradoxes, and explain what you think they add to the play.

Writing Prompts

1. In the form of a short story, write a sequel to *A Midsummer Night's Dream* involving all of its leading characters.

2. Watch any of these three films and write a review of it:
    A Midsummer Night's Sex Comedy (1982); *Dead Poets' Society* (1989);
    A Midsummer Night's Dream (1999).

3. Do some research on any of the following subjects and write a report about your findings.
    *   magic in the Elizabethan era
    *   the origin of fairy stories
    *   the summer solstice (midsummer holiday celebrated in Shakespeare's time)
    *   gender roles in Shakespeare's time
    *   Elizabethan theaters
    *   special effects of the Elizabethan stage

4. Think of your favorite television sitcom, and consider how one of the play's plots might be used to develop an episode of this show. Could Titania's doting on Bottom be adapted for a scene in your sitcom? What about the workmen rehearsing the play? Write a sitcom scene based on one of the plot elements of *A Midsummer Night's Dream*.

5. The English writer Horace Walpole has written, "This world is a comedy to those that think, a tragedy to those that feel." In an essay, respond to this comment, telling whether you agree and why. Explain what this play made you think and/or feel.

Multimodal and Group Activities

1. Set up a contemporary talk show in which the guests are Titania, Lysander, Demetrius, and a specialist in interpreting dreams. Have the host interview the guests about their dreams with the specialist offering interpretations.

2. Divide into two teams, positive and negative, and debate one of the following two resolutions:

   Resolved: Love at first sight is possible.

   Resolved: Love is a decision, not a feeling.

3. Find a work of art based on *A Midsummer Night's Dream*, such as a musical piece, a play, or a painting. In an oral presentation to your group or class, explain how the music, drama, or art captures the mood or events of the play. You may need to use a DVD, CD player, or slides to share this work.

4. In traditional folklore, Puck was portrayed as a demon; in this play, Shakespeare has portrayed him as mostly mischievous. Similarly the story of Pyramus and Thisbe had been considered a tragedy, but Shakespeare turned it into a comedy in the play within the play. Pretend you are a writer interviewing the playwright himself and conduct an interview to find out why Shakespeare made these and other artistic choices. Share your findings.

5. Design costumes for some of the characters in *A Midsummer Night's Dream*. Sketch the garments you design, make replicas for puppets or paper dolls, or use cartoon panels or computer graphics.

6. In groups or individually, go through the script of *A Midsummer Night's Dream* and list all of the places where music cues are needed. Select and record music for all of these moments. Use music of any period, not necessarily the Elizabethan era.

Shakespeare's Life

Many great authors can be imagined as living among the characters in their works. Historical records reveal how these writers spoke, felt, and thought. But Shakespeare is more mysterious. He never gave an interview or wrote an autobiography—not even one of his letters survives. What we know about his life can be told very briefly.

Shakespeare was born in April 1564. The exact date of his birth is unknown, but he was baptized on April 26 in the Stratford-upon-Avon church. His father, John, was a prominent local man who served as town chamberlain and mayor. Young William attended

grammar school in Stratford, where he would have learned Latin—a requirement for a professional career—and some Greek.

In 1582, William married Anne Hathaway. He was 18; she was 26. At the time of their marriage, Anne was already three months pregnant with their first daughter, Susanna. In 1585, the couple had twins, Judith and Hamnet. Hamnet died before reaching adulthood, leaving Shakespeare no male heir.

Even less is known about Shakespeare's life between 1585 and 1592. During that time, he moved to London and became an actor and playwright. He left his family behind in Stratford. Although he surely visited them occasionally, we have little evidence about what Shakespeare was like as a father and a husband.

Several of his early plays were written during this time, including *The Comedy of Errors*, *Titus Andronicus*, and the three parts of *Henry VI*. In those days, working in the theater was rather like acting in soap operas today—the results may be popular, but daytime serials aren't recognized as serious art. In fact, many people were opposed to even allowing plays to be performed. Ministers warned their congregations of the dangers of going to plays.

Queen Elizabeth I

But Shakespeare and his friends were lucky. Queen Elizabeth I loved plays. She protected acting companies from restrictive laws and gave them her permission to perform. Shakespeare wrote several plays to be performed for the queen, including *Twelfth Night*.

After Elizabeth's death in 1603, Shakespeare's company became known as the King's Men. This group of actors performed for James I, who had ruled Scotland before becoming the king of England. Perhaps to thank James for his patronage, Shakespeare wrote *Macbeth*, which included two topics of strong interest to the king—Scottish royalty and witchcraft.

Unlike many theater people, Shakespeare actually earned a good living. By 1599, he was part owner of the Globe, one of the newest theaters in London. Such plays as *Othello*, *Hamlet*, and *King Lear* were first performed there.

In 1610 or 1611, Shakespeare moved back to the familiar surroundings of Stratford-upon-Avon. He was almost 50 years old, well past middle age by 17th-century standards. Over the years, he'd invested in property around Stratford, acquiring a comfortable estate and a family coat of arms.

But Shakespeare didn't give up writing. In 1611, his new play *The Tempest* was performed at court. In 1613, his play *Henry VIII* premiered. This performance was more dramatic than anyone expected. The stage directions called for a cannon to be fired when "King Henry" came on stage. The explosion set the stage on fire, and the entire theater burned to the ground.

Shakespeare died in 1616 at the age of 52. His gravestone carried this inscription:

> **Good friend for Jesus sake forbear**
> **To dig the dust enclosed here!**
> **Blest be the man that spares these stones,**
> **And curst be he that moves my bones.**

This little verse, so crude that it seems unlikely to be Shakespeare's, has intrigued countless scholars and biographers.

Anyone who loves Shakespeare's plays and poems wants to know more about their author. Was he a young man who loved Anne Whateley but was forced into a loveless marriage with another Anne? Did he teach school in Stratford, poach Sir Thomas Lucy's deer, or work for a lawyer in London? Who is the "dark lady" of his sonnets?

But perhaps we are fortunate in our ignorance. Orson Welles, who directed an all-black stage production of *Macbeth* in 1936, put it this way: "Luckily, we know almost nothing about Shakespeare . . . and that makes it so much easier to understand [his] works . . . It's an egocentric, romantic, 19th-century conception that the artist is more interesting and more important than his art."

In Shakespeare's world, there can be little question of which is truly important, the work or the author. Shakespeare brings up the curtain and then steps back into the wings, trusting the play to a cast of characters so stunningly vivid that they sometimes seem more real than life.

Shakespeare's Theater

In Shakespeare's London, a day's entertainment often began with a favorite amusement, bearbaiting. A bear would be captured and chained to a stake inside a pit. A pack of dogs would be released, and they would attack the bear. Spectators placed bets on which would die first. Admission to these pits cost only a penny, so they were very popular with working-class Londoners.

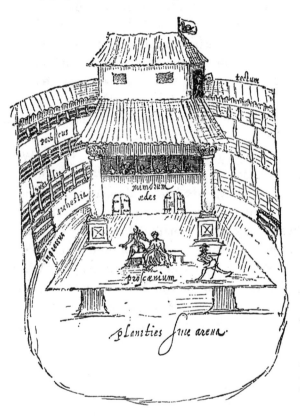

The Swan Theatre in London, drawn in 1596, the only known contemporary image of an Elizabethan theater interior

After the bearbaiting was over, another penny purchased admission to a play. Each theater had its own company of actors, often supported by a nobleman or a member of the royal family. For part of his career, Shakespeare was a member of the Lord

Chamberlain's Men. After the death of Queen Elizabeth I, King James I became the patron of Shakespeare's company. The actors became known as the King's Men.

As part owner of the Globe Theatre, Shakespeare wrote plays, hired actors, and paid the bills. Since the Globe presented a new play every three weeks, Shakespeare and his actors had little time to rehearse or polish their productions. To complicate matters even more, most actors played more than one part in a play.

Boys played all the female roles. Most acting companies had three or four youths who were practically raised in the theater. They started acting as early as age seven and played female roles until they began shaving. Shakespeare had a favorite boy actor (probably named John Rice) who played Cleopatra and Lady Macbeth. Actresses would not become part of the English theater for another fifty years.

Richard Tarleton, Elizabethan actor famous for his clowning

The audience crowded into the theater at about 2 p.m. The cheapest seats weren't seats at all but standing room in front of the stage. This area, known as the "pit," was occupied by "groundlings" or "penny knaves," who could be more trouble to the actors than they were worth. If the play was boring, the groundlings would throw rotten eggs or vegetables. They talked loudly to their friends, played cards, and even picked fights with each other. One theater was set on fire by audience members who didn't like the play.

The theater was open to the sky, so rain or snow presented a problem. However, the actors were partially protected by a roof known as the "heavens," and wealthier patrons sat in three stories of sheltered galleries that surrounded the pit and most of the main stage.

The main stage, about 25 feet deep and 45 feet wide, projected into the audience, so spectators were closely involved in the action. This stage was rather bare, with only a few pieces of furniture. But this simplicity allowed for flexible and fluid staging. Unlike too many later productions, plays at the Globe did not grind to a halt for scene changes. When one group of actors exited through one doorway and a new group entered through another, Shakespeare's audience understood that a new location was probably being represented.

Behind the main stage was the "tiring-house," where the actors changed costumes. Above the stage was a gallery that, when it wasn't occupied by musicians or wealthy patrons, could suggest any kind of high place—castle ramparts, a cliff, or a balcony.

Special effects were common. A trap door in the main stage allowed ghosts to appear. Even more spectacularly, supernatural beings could be lowered from above the stage. For added realism, actors hid bags of pig's blood and guts under their stage doublets. When pierced with a sword, the bags spilled out over the stage and produced a gory effect.

All these staging methods and design elements greatly appealed to Elizabethan audiences and made plays increasingly popular. By the time Shakespeare died in 1616, there were more than thirty theaters in and around London.

What would Shakespeare, so accustomed to the rough-and-tumble stagecraft of the Globe, think of the theaters where his plays are performed today? He would probably miss some of the vitality of the Globe. For centuries now, his plays have been most often performed on stages with a frame called the "proscenium arch," which cleanly separates the audience from the performers. This barrier tends to cast a peculiar shroud of privacy over his plays so that his characters do not seem to quite enter our world.

But with greater and greater frequency, Shakespeare's plays are being performed out-of-doors or in theaters with three- or four-sided stages. And a replica of the Globe Theatre itself opened in London in 1996, only about 200 yards from the site of the original.

The new Globe Theatre, London

This new Globe is an exciting laboratory where directors and actors can test ideas about Elizabethan staging. Their experiments may change our ideas about how Shakespeare's plays were performed and give new insights into their meaning.

The Globe Theatre

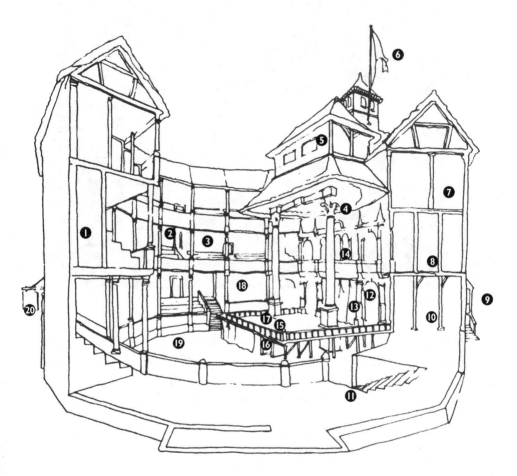

1 **Corridor** A passageway serving the middle gallery.

2 **Entrance** Point leading to the staircase and upper galleries.

3 **Middle Gallery** The seats here were higher priced.

4 **The Heavens** So identified by being painted with the zodiac signs.

5 **Hut** A storage area that also held a winch system for lowering characters to the stage.

6 **Flag** A white flag above the theater meant a show that day.

7 **Wardrobe** A storage area for costumes and props.

8 **Dressing Rooms** Rooms where actors were "attired" and awaited their cues.

9 **Tiring-House Door** The rear entrance or "stage door" for actors or privileged spectators.

10 **Tiring-House** Backstage area providing space for storage and costume changes.

11 **Stairs** Theatergoers reached the galleries by staircases enclosed by stairwells.

12 **Stage Doors** Doors opening into the Tiring-House.

13 **Inner Stage** A recessed playing area often curtained off except as needed.

14 **Gallery** Located above the stage to house musicians or spectators.

15 **Trap Door** Leading to the "Hell" area, where a winch elevator was located.

16 **Hell** The area under the stage, used for ghostly comings and goings or for storage.

17 **Stage** Major playing area jutting into the Pit, creating a sense of intimacy.

18 **Lords Rooms** or private galleries. Six pennies let a viewer sit here, or sometimes on stage.

19 **The Pit** Sometimes referred to as "The Yard," where the "groundlings" watched.

20 **Main Entrance** Here the doorkeeper collected admission.

IMAGE CREDITS